CW00481409

HOW TO DESIGN A TRAINING COL

Also available from Continuum:

The Agricultural Science Teachers' Handbook – Peter Taylor
The English Language Teacher's Handbook – Joanna Baker and
    Heather Westrup
Essential Speaking Skills – Joanna Baker and Heather Westrup

How to Design a Training Course

A guide to participatory
curriculum development

Peter Taylor

**Sharing skills
Changing lives**

continuum
LONDON • NEW YORK

Continuum   **VSO**
The Tower Building   15 East 26th Street   317 Putney Bridge Road
11 York Road   New York   London
London SE1 7NX   NY 10010   SW15 2PN

First published by Continuum in 2003

British Library Cataloguing-in-Publication Data
A catalogue record for this book is available from the British Library.

ISBN: 0–8264–5694–4 (hardback)
        0–8264–5695–2 (paperback)

Illustrations by Dandi Palmer © VSO/Dandi Palmer.
Cover images © VSO/Spaull (top left, top right, bottom left); © VSO/Gary John
Norman (bottom middle); © VSO/Annie Sloan (bottom right).

Typeset by Kenneth Burnley, Wirral, Cheshire
Printed and bound in Great Britain by Cromwell Press Ltd, Trowbridge, Wiltshire

Contents

Acknowledgements

This book would not have been possible without contributions and assistance from a number of people. Silke Bernau once again proved an excellent, insightful and dedicated editor, complemented by great support from Penny Amerena and Lara Carim, all from VSO Books. Participatory and partnership approaches are key to VSO's development work. Three VSO volunteers, Julia Sander, Alexandra Schomburg and Valerie Blackwell participated in action research with their local colleagues to test the ideas and methods on which this book is based, and shared their experiences and thoughts on how to make things work in many different ways. This VSO experience is woven throughout the book and provides valuable insight into participatory curriculum development in action with stakeholders.

Many other practitioners have provided inspiration and have tested the concepts and approaches provided in this book in real contexts. Abdil Segisbaev and colleagues of the Helvetas Agricultural and Rural Vocational Education Project in Kyrgyzstan provided some excellent case study material, demonstrating what participatory curriculum development can mean in practice. Markus Arbenz and Bardolf Paul both helped to create environments in which participation could flourish. Many lessons were learned from Vietnamese and Swiss colleagues in the Helvetas Social Forestry Support Programme in Vietnam. Per Rudebjer, Joe Peters and Lydia Braakman have all demonstrated that friendship and professional interest in participation in education and training can be combined. Jan Beniest of ICRAF and Hans Schaltenbrand of Helvetas have continued to encourage the use of a PCD approach in various contexts around the world. Robert Chambers, John Gaventa, Jethro Pettit at the Institute of Development Studies and their many collaborators continue to promote participation and participatory teaching and learning, both in theory and practice. A wide range of people, farmers, students, teachers, parents, writers, researchers, who cannot all be named here, have themselves participated and brought along their amazing energy and enthusiasm on numerous occasions. Gratitude goes to all of you.

Finally, special thanks go to Mary, Sorcha and Meadhbh. Without your support, this book would probably not have been started, and certainly would not have been completed.

Introduction

Training is an important part of many development programmes. Good training enables participants to gain new knowledge and skills as well as the attitudes which will help them to put these into practice to change their situations.

There is increasing concern, however, that many training courses are not effective. They do not enable participants to gain useful new knowledge and the skills and attitudes to apply it. This means that the behaviour of the learners is unlikely to change, so the outcome of the training is not useful or sustainable.

As a result, many organizations are now paying more attention to how they plan, design, deliver and evaluate their training courses. Many trainers now recognize that this cycle of curriculum development is a vital element in the success of education and training.

Participatory curriculum development (PCD) is an emerging approach which builds on the many success stories of participation in development programmes. There is growing evidence from many countries that a PCD approach improves the effectiveness and sustainability of training courses by creating partnerships between trainers, participants and others who have an interest in the training and its outcomes.

The demand for training designed using a PCD approach is increasing rapidly. There is also a growing need for trainers who can use a PCD approach effectively in a range of learning contexts. This book will provide you with clear guidance on how you can use the participatory curriculum development approach in your work.

Look at these three examples of learning contexts: they are all within the scope of this book, demonstrating that PCD can be used in different situations, at different levels and in different forms of education and training.

Example 1: Learning informally

Children learn how to talk, walk and eat without attending any training. They observe others who are doing these things, and keep trying until they can do them successfully. A farmer who has grown maize for many years can tell when maize cobs are ready to harvest by feeling them, with no formal training. She may have observed older family members many times and tried to copy what they did, or maybe she learned as a result of picking cobs at different times and finding out which was the right time.

Example 2: Learning by coaching: apprenticeship in carpentry

A young man wanted to become a carpenter. He found an experienced carpenter nearby who took him on as an apprentice. Every day, the young man watched the master carpenter carry out different tasks. Then the trainee tried to copy the expert. When the trainee made a mistake, the expert gave advice on what went wrong. When the trainee did a good job, the expert usually praised the trainee. After repeating the exercise several times, the trainee could carry out the task quite easily. They used the same approach for many different carpentry tasks. The expert gave advice and demonstrations to the trainee. Eventually, the trainee could carry out the different carpentry tasks almost without thinking. After two years, when both he and the expert carpenter were satisfied with his ability, the young man started his own business as a carpenter. There was enough demand for both carpenters to earn a good living from their work.

Example 3: Learning on a formal training course

The government was concerned because many children and adults in rural areas attended the district clinics with diarrhoea, internal parasites and general ill health. A consultant advised the Minister for Health that these problems often arise from poor hygiene in food preparation and the government decided that a major national campaign was needed to improve hygiene in rural areas. An important part of this campaign was a series of training events for community health workers. The planners in the capital city decided that the training courses would be held in the sixth month of the national campaign. The course was designed by academics and health experts from the Training Department of the Ministry of Health. It included a lot of theory topics, such as the types of disease organism, how diseases are transmitted and the function of the immune system in the human body. It took longer than expected to write the course, so the curriculum reached the provincial health officers only a few days before the course started. Since the planners had decided that the courses would last for two weeks, the health officers in each province had announced that community health workers from all villages would come to a training centre in the provincial capital. Some health workers arrived late, because it took so long to travel to the provincial city. Some did not come at all, because the sixth month of the campaign was the main harvesting season. The curriculum was new to the trainers, so they spent a lot of time on the theory topics, which were the main part of the course. There was a lot to cover, so the trainers had to explain most topics very quickly, with little time for questions. Only three days were left for practical sessions on hygiene and food preparation. These were done by the trainers on the old electric appliances in the small kitchens of the training centre. As the kitchens were small, the health workers took turns to watch the demonstration. There was no assessment of what the health workers learned, but an end-of-course evaluation was carried out. All the participants who completed the course received a certificate.

Figure 1: Learning informally

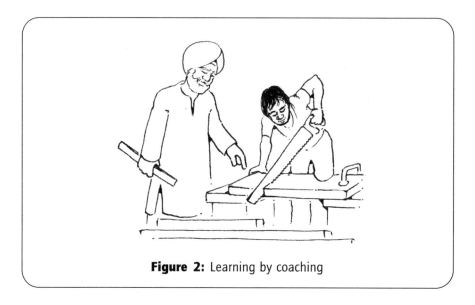

Figure 2: Learning by coaching

Figure 3: Learning on a formal training course

What do you think about these examples? They are all imaginary, but they could have been from real life. In this book, you will read about real case studies, and a framework and tools which will help you to ensure that your own training programmes are effective. (The last example contains hints about some of the factors which have an impact on the effectiveness of a training course. Maybe you spotted most of them.)

This book will help you

▶ to use participatory curriculum development (PCD) to design more effective training courses
▶ to involve trainers, potential trainees and stakeholders
▶ to provide leadership, facilitation, training and coaching in all aspects of the PCD cycle
▶ to design, implement and evaluate more effective training programmes.

Even if you have excellent technical knowledge and skills in your area of expertise, this book will help you to improve your ability to manage and facilitate processes, and to deliver training effectively.

The book provides you with a structured approach which guides you through the key phases of the PCD cycle and some concrete practical methods and tools. We give concrete and practical tips and tools so that you can adapt the PCD cycle to your local context wherever you are in the world. There are hints on how to avoid common problems, and suggestions for overcoming constraints.

We hope this book will help you and your colleagues to learn and to train more effectively. But remember that this book is not a blueprint or a recipe: it is a guide which you can adapt to your situation and needs. We asked three VSO trainers and curriculum developers to use the PCD cycle in their work in an action research project for this book. They recorded what they did, what they adapted and what the outcomes were. Throughout the book, short case studies from their experience show you how they adapted the PCD cycle to their own situations. We hope this will help you to see how you can apply PCD in your own work.

The book also draws on the extensive experience of the author and of VSO and national trainers, and there are many examples from different contexts and fields of development.

WHO THIS BOOK IS FOR

This book is for all development professionals who are involved in training, curriculum development and human resource development, no matter what your context or field of specialism.

You may work for a non-government organization, a government ministry or programme, an international project or donor, or you may work in a school or other education institution, in a non-formal training programme, or in a curriculum development unit.

The PCD cycle is useful if you are a community extension worker, a teacher or lecturer, a subject or technical specialist, or a worker in pre-service and in-service training institutions. You will find it useful in any fields of specialism, including agriculture, forestry, fisheries, health and nutrition, education, and community and rural development.

It can also help you if you are involved more generally in promoting participation and facilitation skills, and in developing education and training programmes.

The case studies in this book are taken from a range of institutional settings, which show how different challenges and strategies can be addressed.

HOW TO USE THIS BOOK

Part I looks at the big issues that surround training, and the wide range of processes, methods and personal skills necessary for participatory curriculum development, including facilitation, communication and networking. It introduces the basic principles of PCD and we look briefly at the main phases of the PCD cycle.

We then consider in more detail what we mean by curriculum development, why it is important for learning and why learning and training should be participatory. This will help you to see the benefits of PCD. We think about who should participate in curriculum development, and give some examples of real cases where a participatory approach to curriculum development has been used. We also look at some of the challenges that you may face and suggest concrete ways to help you overcome them.

Also in Part I, we focus on the training and learning processes. We discuss how and why learning takes place, what makes learning effective and what may block effective learning. We offer practical guidance on how you can facilitate learning. We also consider how course design leads to learning and change, what an effective training course should look like, and how you can monitor and evaluate the success of a training course.

All of this will prepare you for Part II, where you will find clear guidelines on how to carry out a process of participatory curriculum development successfully.

Part I
Participatory Curriculum
Development and Learning –
some key concepts
and issues

Section 1: Participatory curriculum development

WHAT IS PARTICIPATORY CURRICULUM DEVELOPMENT?

Participatory curriculum development (PCD) builds upon the many success stories of participation in rural development programmes. There is growing evidence from experience in a range of countries that a PCD approach improves the effectiveness and sustainability of course design and training. It

► creates working partnerships between trainers and other stakeholders
► increases ownership of the complete training process
► improves the potential for effective learning through participation.

PCD is not only about writing the curriculum, it deals with participation in the entire training cycle. This book, therefore, uses a wider definition of curriculum development than you may be used to.

Let's start by examining some of the main concepts of the PCD cycle.

WHAT IS CURRICULUM DEVELOPMENT?

What do we mean by curriculum development? Start by reflecting on your own experience. Perhaps you already have experience of designing and delivering training courses. If so, before you read further, try to answer the following questions:

► What does curriculum development mean to you?
► What experience do you have of curriculum development?
► What have you learned from this experience?
► What have others who were involved learned from this experience?

What were your answers? Perhaps, when you saw the word 'curriculum', you thought of a formal classroom, and a resource like a book or a thick pile of paper with lists, tables and diagrams. Or perhaps you thought of a small group of people sitting in an office writing a document which will be sent out to teachers all over the country: or maybe you thought about the resources which are needed for curriculum development to take place.

Figure I.1.1: People or paper?

You may like to read a definition of curriculum development, and to compare your own experience and ideas with what is provided in this book. In fact, it is difficult to give a definition, because curriculum development depends a lot on the context in which it happens.

However, in every context, we should think of curriculum development as a continuous and flexible process. So, here is a description of curriculum development, rather than a definition. This description is the basis for the PCD cycle described in this book:

> Curriculum development describes all the ways in which a training or teaching organization plans and guides learning. This learning can take place in groups or with individual learners. It can take place inside or outside a classroom. It can take place in an institutional setting like a school, college or training centre, or in a village or a field. Curriculum development is central to the teaching and learning process.
>
> (From Rogers and Taylor, 1998)

So you can see that curriculum development can take place in many settings, and may involve many people. Is this idea similar to your own?

In curriculum development, there are **four** main things which you need to do if you want your training courses to be effective:

1. Identify what learners want or need to know and decide what type of training can meet their learning needs.
2. Plan the training so that learning is likely to take place.
3. Deliver the training so that learning does take place.
4. Evaluate the training so that there is evidence that learning has taken place.

This book will stress that **all** these things should be done in a participatory way, not only the delivery of the training (although that is also important).

After you have read this book, you should be able to identify who should participate in the entire training process. You should also be able to plan, deliver and evaluate your training using a participatory approach.

But why should curriculum development be participatory? Let's look at that now.

WHY SHOULD CURRICULUM DEVELOPMENT BE PARTICIPATORY?

You will find some real benefits if you use a participatory approach to curriculum development. First and foremost, the training you provide, and the learning of all participants, will become more effective. Why is that? As an example let's first think about something with which you are probably very familiar: the delivery of the training. No doubt you have experienced training as a participant at some time in your life, and possibly also delivered some training programmes. Look at the two illustrations in Figure I.1.2.

Does Scene 1 look familiar to you? It is very common. We can describe it by saying that this training is about what the trainer wants to tell. The trainer has decided what the trainees need to know and tries to transfer this knowledge to the learners. The learners are not asked to do anything other than to listen. Maybe sometimes they ask a question, which the trainer will answer. In such a learning context, not much real learning will take place. Perhaps some people will learn that training can be a very boring activity. How does this scene compare with training courses you have experienced, either as a trainer, or as a participant?

Figure I.1.2: Two training scenes

In Scene 2, you can see that the learners as well as the trainer are actively participating. We can describe it by saying that this training is about what the learners want to know. Learners are motivated to learn if they identify what their learning needs are, if they are involved in deciding how their learning needs can be met, and if they participate actively during the training. This means that the training is more likely to be effective.

We believe there should be participation during the *entire* curriculum development cycle. Here are some of the benefits you will find if you work in a more participatory way:

▶ You should have more opportunities for discussion and reflection with learners and stakeholders (different people and groups who have an interest in the training). This will help everyone learn and work together more effectively.

▶ You should be able to form links with other organizations and networks more easily, so that you can share information better. Your courses should become more relevant to the local context.

▶ Groups and individuals who might not normally have a voice, such as women, poor people or children, will benefit more from training.

▶ You should be able to establish a dynamic course design process as new lines of communication develop, resulting in greater satisfaction with your training programmes.

▶ Stakeholders gain greater responsibility for stages of the curriculum development cycle. This increases the motivation and commitment of everyone who participates.

We can summarize all these benefits by saying that if you use a participatory curriculum development approach, your training will be more effective, and the benefits – the learning which takes place and the change in behaviour which results – will be more sustainable.

With benefits like these, you might expect participatory curriculum development to be a very common approach. Unfortunately, the evidence shows that many people, especially in rural areas, are involved very little in the development of education and training programmes which affect them directly. (Think back to the training course in the third learning example on pages 2–3. Where was it designed and by whom?)

Where participatory approaches have been used, the benefits have been seen: greater ownership by everyone involved, better solutions to complex problems, and more sustainable outcomes. Here are some examples from south-east Asia.

PCD in forestry education in Cambodia

Two key forestry education institutions in Cambodia realized the need to transform their training programmes to meet the needs of the national economy and the many Cambodian people who depend on forests for their income. The ownership, sustainable management and use of forest land is of critical importance. Instead of the traditional top-down approach to training-course design, the forestry institutes, with the support of several international agencies, started a participatory curriculum development cycle with awareness-raising workshops. These workshops enabled teachers to understand better the relationship between how the curriculum is developed and effective learning, and to recognize the importance of involving different stakeholders in the cycle upon which they were embarking. The journey of educational change based on participation will be long in Cambodia, but the enthusiasm and commitment of teachers generated by the workshops has ensured that it has begun.

> ## Using PCD to design an education project in Vietnam
>
> The provincial authorities requested Helvetas, a Swiss NGO, to support the development of a vocational school specializing in agriculture and forestry in Cao Bang province. This school wanted to revise its curriculum completely and the teachers needed training to enable them to do this. Rather than using a traditional top-down approach to planning, a participatory workshop was organized, which combined elements of PCD and organizational development. A wide range of stakeholders was invited, including teachers, students, govern-ment officials, extension workers, project representatives and farmers. Groups were formed for various aspects of the planning: the farmer group gave their own inputs into the planning process. The farmers' voices were heard to the extent that the entire project design was turned around. The teachers realized that they had to meet the learning needs of the farmers, and the curriculum was based on their clearly-articulated training needs. It was an opportunity to see the meaning of demand-driven training in action.

So why are participatory approaches not used more often? One reason is that real participation takes time. If you are gaining input and agreement from a wide range of people, it takes longer to agree something than if a few trainers sit in a room and agree everything among themselves.

Another major reason is that real participation means sharing power: power over resources, decision-making and outcomes. Many people and organiza-tions find it difficult to share power and its benefits. Sometimes this is because they think they will lose some benefits themselves. But more often it is because they have never really thought about participation in practice.

This book will show that if you use a participatory approach to curriculum development, training is much more likely to be effective. You will be able to help more people to learn more useful things, so that they can use what they have learned for the benefit of themselves and others. So everyone, including you, will gain.

Maybe now you have some questions about participation. How much should someone participate at any one particular time? And who should participate? When you set up a participatory curriculum development cycle, you need to decide all these things. We will now discuss this in more detail, and you will find out how to put it into practice in Part II.

WHO PARTICIPATES AND WHY? THE INVOLVEMENT OF STAKEHOLDERS IN PCD

So far, we have identified two groups involved in training courses: the trainers and the learners. But what about other participants in the overall process of training and learning? Think about the answers to these questions:

▶ Who has participated in the design of training courses in which you have been involved?
▶ Why did they participate?
▶ Who decided they should participate?
▶ What did they gain?
▶ What did they contribute?

The groups and individuals who have an interest or claim in any process are called *stakeholders*. Stakeholders feel they should have some ownership of the process: and they are also people who may benefit from being involved in the process. Think back to the third learning example on pages 2–3. The stakeholders here include the community health workers, the provincial health officers, the academics and staff at the training department of the Ministry of Health and the Minister. Can you think of others?

In training, there are many different stakeholders. External stakeholders or outsiders come from outside the institution or immediate setting where the training is designed and delivered. Internal stakeholders or insiders come from within the institution or setting. Here are some examples of outsider and insider stakeholders in a training programme:

Outsiders	Insiders
Policy-makers	Training organization administrators and managers
Politicians and national educational administrators	Teachers and trainers
Educational experts	Learners/trainees/students
Employer/professional bodies	Curriculum writers
Clients, e.g. farmers, parents, community members, etc.	Auxiliary and support staff, e.g. technicians, field staff, etc.
Funders	
Former students	
Interest groups, e.g. NGOs, religious organizations, etc	
Parents	
Book publishers	

Figure I.1.3: In training, there are many different stakeholders

Every context has its own stakeholders, although those mentioned in the table are quite typical. You will need to identify the stakeholders who have an interest in your training. Later in this book, you will learn how to carry out a stakeholder analysis.

Here are some important points about stakeholders and identifying what their interest is:

▶ Different stakeholders have different interests (claims or gains). Some stakeholders, such as policy-makers, have a general interest, while others, for example employers, may have a very specific interest.
▶ Some stakeholders, for example the trainers and the learners, are interested in the process of training (such as how the course is taught). Other stakeholders, such as government officials and parents, may be more interested in the product or outcome (how many students graduate). Learners and trainers are probably interested in both process and product.

▶ Many stakeholders may be very supportive of the training approach. Others may be less supportive, for example, managers who feel they have limited funds available. Occasionally, some stakeholders are hostile, particularly if there is direct competition between institutions or even between individuals.

▶ Some stakeholders are very open about their interest. These stakeholders are more straightforward to work with, regardless of whether they support or oppose the training. Other stakeholders may not reveal their true opinions, for example, for strategic reasons or sometimes because of cultural beliefs. This is one reason why participatory curriculum development can become a long and dynamic process.

▶ The list of stakeholders may change over time, as the context changes, or as the nature of the training changes. You will need to monitor the situation to ensure that all relevant stakeholders are involved. You will find out how to do this later in this book.

WHY IS PARTICIPATION NEEDED?

This is a big question. There is a lot of debate about what participation really means, and whether there is a strong, identifiable theory which underpins the nature of participation. We could easily fill this book with a discussion on this issue alone, but this is not the book's purpose. Here are a few key points to remember about participation:

▶ Participation is not only a means but also an end in itself.

▶ Poor and marginalized people have a right to take part in decision-making which affects their lives. This will only happen if many people in society change their behaviour, attitudes and power relationships. Education and training have an important role to play in this type of change.

▶ Greater participation can help to reduce poverty and social injustice. It has a role to play in nation-building. It can do this by strengthening the rights and voice of citizens, by influencing policy-making, by enhancing local governance and by improving the accountability and responsiveness of institutions.

▶ Participatory approaches are spreading widely throughout the world, but some people fear that they are often applied only to please donors and government agencies.

▶ There is a growing need for people who are active, interested and open to the meaning, methods and practice of participation.

▶ In education, participation can be found in initiatives such as:
- community-based learning
- participatory curriculum development
- popular education
- experiential learning
- distance learning
- initiatives which increase access to education.

▶ More and more education and training institutions around the world are encouraging participatory teaching and learning processes, forming links with communities, and building a more participatory curriculum development process. They find that this makes teaching and learning more effective.

▶ Your learners will be strongly influenced by the way you work and teach. If you are participatory, the chances are that they will be too. This will benefit you, them, their local communities and society in general. This is probably the strongest reason for following a participatory approach in learning and teaching.

You may be feeling nervous about setting off on a journey which involves approaches which may be new to you and a lot of stakeholders. Fortunately, there are many examples from those who have used and tried this approach. For this book, we asked a VSO trainer in Malawi and a VSO curriculum developer in The Gambia to use the PCD cycle with their national colleagues. Here are their first experiences.

So far, we met stakeholders from all sides and did a needs assessment. We couldn't bring them all together at one time to one place because of lacking resources. Instead of them coming to us, we combined trips. Where we realized that different groups or organizations could benefit/learn from each other, we linked them up to exchange their experiences. All meetings were absolutely satisfying, since there is a learning aspect on both sides and we got brilliant feedback from farmers' groups, extension workers and donor agencies. We are busy writing the draft manual [a Food Processing Extension Manual] now. Combined with the pilot training course, there will be a first review of the manual, with the involvement of stakeholders. The reviewed manual will be field tested afterwards in different areas all over Malawi. A final workshop with stakeholders is planned to get feedback from the field experience with the manual and to do the last necessary corrections to the material.

VSO trainer, Malawi, 2001

Although I succeeded in seeing the key stakeholders individually, I was not able to bring them together for a workshop. Communication between the stakeholders is vital if everyone's aspirations are to be fulfilled. It is difficult to establish channels of communication here – in fact frequently people claim that they have not been informed even when this is not the case! It would be so much better if we could all get together at the outset!

VSO curriculum developer, The Gambia, 2001

WHAT DOES PARTICIPATION MEAN IN PRACTICE?

Participation is often thought of as a good thing, but as the second example above shows, it is not easy to achieve. It helps if you build up a set of principles which you can follow in order to stay on the right track. There is no ready-made list of principles which apply in all situations, but the following points may help you set up your own list.

1. The curriculum development process does not have to be dominated by one group or individual. We should aim for joint leadership, although someone will need to make the final decisions.
2. Everyone looks at the world differently. We need to respect these different views and find out where our views coincide with the views of others.
3. All stakeholders have something to contribute. We need to find out how to help them make their contribution easily and effectively.
4. Each person builds his/her own knowledge. We need to respect the knowledge and experience of others and share these with our own. Learning then becomes synergistic – building new knowledge together.
5. Participation is active and involves different people practising or learning by doing. As a result of participating, a person's knowledge will change.
6. As well as learning through their knowledge and practice, different stakeholders hold different values, attitudes and beliefs. We need to understand these and take them into consideration when we share ideas with others.
7. Every context is different. We should try to understand every situation, and to accept that it is complex. This can be achieved by involving those who know their own situation best.

Can you add some more principles of your own? If you discuss these principles with other colleagues or stakeholders, you may be surprised at what you develop.

CHALLENGES FOR PARTICIPATORY CURRICULUM DEVELOPMENT

We have already mentioned that if you increase participation in curriculum development, training and learning should become more effective. This sounds wonderful. Of course, life is rarely simple, and you may face some challenges when you become more participatory. Some people see these challenges as a reason to avoid a participatory approach, and to believe that participation is a nice idea but too difficult to do in practice.

Experience shows, however, that many challenges can be overcome. In this book, we want to be pragmatic. As a teacher once said, 'We need to change our stumbling blocks into stepping stones'! Here are a few stumbling blocks you might encounter, as well as some ideas on how to overcome them. Later in this book you will find even more practical ways to do this.

Challenges you might face	How you might overcome them
Some stakeholders may have unrealistic expectations at an early stage and these may not be met.	Establish a platform where you can have an open discussion or dialogue with different stakeholders. Try to make this non-threatening and constructive.
Involving stakeholders may be costly in terms of their time and effort, especially where they have very few resources or low income.	Find out the reality of costs and resources needed for participation. Resources often exist which are untapped. Provide resources in a clear and transparent way, according to clear guidelines.
Sometimes stakeholders feel that they have been invited as a 'token gesture', just to gain approval from some other agency such as a donor.	Always be clear about why a particular stakeholder is invited to participate. Provide all necessary information, and take time to discuss with different groups what their role might be.
Bringing groups of people together has logistical implications which may be beyond the capacity of the training organizers.	Plan events carefully. If necessary, go to the people rather than bringing people to you. Try to coincide your own events with others where many of the stakeholders will be present.
Creating a mechanism by which different stakeholders can work and interact on an equal basis is complex due to different perceptions, experience, educational	Do not assume that all stakeholders have the same interests. Explain exactly what you hope to achieve and find out what their views are. Whenever possible, help different stakeholders to identify their own needs and the ways in which those needs might be addressed through a

Challenges you might face	*How you might overcome them*
backgrounds and understanding of the wider course design process.	joint effort. In some cases, certain stakeholders may remain disinterested. If all efforts fail, you may have to accept that you cannot involve those stakeholders at that time. Work with those who are interested; maybe the others will decide to join in later.
Participation is demanding on time and resources. This may alienate some policy-makers, donors and practitioners.	Set up a platform for discussion with all stakeholders. Hold special discussions with key decision-makers, and ensure that they are informed regularly. Explain the aims of the process openly and honestly and emphasize that although the process may take longer than normal, the outcomes should be better and more sustainable.
Training-course developers often think that they know best, and may not value the opinions of some stakeholders, especially rural people. Trainers may be unaware of the reality of the rural context and lack field-based experience.	Accept that you cannot know everything. It is by sharing ideas with others and learning from them that you will work more effectively. The more you are prepared to learn, the more you will be able to offer to others.
Some stakeholders are suspicious or feel intimidated by the training course developers because they think they are really looking for other types of information, or because they have experienced training which was not useful.	Having a platform for discussion should help to overcome this difficulty. Encourage people to be open about their fears as well as their expectations.
Some potential trainees are not sure of their training needs and are not aware of the possibilities for training.	As a trainer, you are in a position to give some concrete input and advice. This is your job after all. But your input must suit the local context and the needs of the learners. You need to understand these before your own input can be of value. Try to master some basic methods and tools which will help you to find out what is needed (you will be helped with this later in this book).
Discussions about training needs are dominated by certain powerful groups, such as rich farmers or male farmers, at the expense of poor farmers and women farmers.	As you begin to understand the situation better, you may decide to bring different groups together at different times, to avoid domination by some groups over others. You may need to mediate or help people to resolve their conflicts. Although it is never good to get involved in local 'politics', it is important always to remember that education is never 'neutral'. There may be times when you have to give active support to groups who are marginalized or oppressed.

Challenges you might face	How you might overcome them
There are shortages of resources and logistical problems in involving farmers in a meaningful way. Poor people may not be able to afford the potential loss in production or income by spending time away from their work.	Try to understand and respect the realities of the lives of those you would like to work with. Spend time finding out about their lives and work, and try to arrange events and activities at times when most people can attend without too much difficulty.

The PCD cycle – a framework for action

Figure I.1.4 is a framework (based on a model developed by Skilbeck) which illustrates how the phases of participatory curriculum development fit together. This framework will help you because it does two main things. It contains a series of phases you can follow, and also it shows that participatory curriculum development is a cycle.

Each phase (1 to 5) of the cycle involves a number of activities. Which activities you do depend on your context – for example, whether you work in a formal education institution or on an informal village extension programme – and on whether you are the trainer, the course designer, a manager or a facilitator. Part 2 of this book discusses the activities for each phase in detail and gives you practical tools for putting them into practice.

The arrows linking each part of the cycle show the direction in which it normally goes. Typically, you start by analysing the situation, then move through the phases of planning, detailed course design, course delivery and evaluation. All the stages are related to each other, so if one part changes, you may need to adapt the other stages as well. And in the centre of the cycle is the important focus on stakeholder involvement which is the core of PCD.

An important point demonstrated by this diagram is that PCD is a continuous cycle, not a line where evaluation takes place when you reach the end point. It is important to develop a monitoring and evaluation system at an early stage; do not leave evaluation to the end. Sadly, a book cannot be circular, so we cover ideas about monitoring and evaluation near the end, on pages 134–52. You might like to take a look at that section of the book now before moving on.

Finally, the broad arrows outside the cycle are there to remind us that there is often a need for support and stimulation to maintain the momentum of the PCD cycle so it does not grind to a halt. You may have a key role in ensuring that the PCD cycle keeps evolving as long as it is needed.

Different versions of this cycle have been used by many people involved in curriculum development. Here is one example from Nepal.

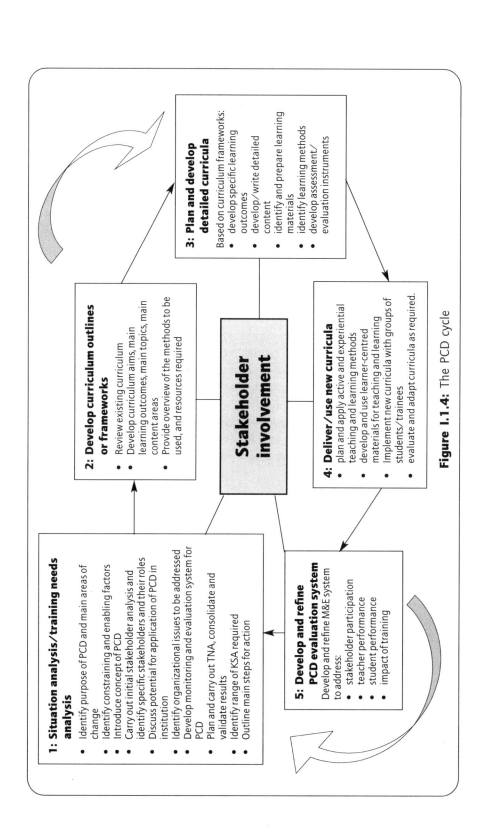

1: Situation analysis/training needs analysis

- Identify purpose of PCD and main areas of change
- Identify constraining and enabling factors
- Introduce concept of PCD
- Carry out initial stakeholder analysis and identify specific stakeholders and their roles
- Discuss potential for application of PCD in institution
- Identify organizational issues to be addressed
- Develop monitoring and evaluation system for PCD
- Plan and carry out TNA, consolidate and validate results
- Identify range of KSA required
- Outline main steps for action

2: Develop curriculum outlines or frameworks

- Review existing curriculum
- Develop curriculum aims, main learning outcomes, main topics, main content areas
- Provide overview of the methods to be used, and resources required

3: Plan and develop detailed curricula

Based on curriculum frameworks:
- develop specific learning outcomes
- develop/write detailed content
- identify and prepare learning materials
- identify learning methods
- develop assessment/evaluation instruments

Stakeholder involvement

4: Deliver/use new curricula

- plan and apply active and experiential teaching and learning methods
- develop and use learner-centred materials for teaching and learning
- implement new curricula with groups of students/trainees
- evaluate and adapt curricula as required.

5: Develop and refine PCD evaluation system

Develop and refine M&E system to address:
- stakeholder participation
- teacher performance
- student performance
- impact of training

Figure I.1.4: The PCD cycle

Experience of using the cycle in PCD for a workshop on updating the forest guards course in Nepal

The use of [Skilbeck's] model helped the process of curriculum development. The basic pragmatic questions that the model forced the participants to ask helped focus on the key issues involved. The other major value of using the Skilbeck model lay in the way it helped structure the workshop participants' thinking around the delivery of the learning experiences for the Forestry Guard trainees. When trying to teach such topics as communication skills, the method of delivery becomes as important as the content . . . The workshop methodology enabled a considerable amount of participation; the workshop participants chose the workshop priorities, the objectives of the new curriculum (based upon recognized and agreed training needs), the content and teaching methods to be used and the actions then required in order to swiftly implement the new curriculum. The adult education workshop methodology used also enabled senior staff to comfortably listen to field staff who were often younger and/or junior in rank. Finally, but perhaps most importantly, the workshop methodology allowed a true sense of ownership of the new curriculum to develop. All the staff involved in the first workshop felt that they had participated in a practical and time-efficient process that enabled the training methods and content of the Forestry Guards curriculum to catch up with forestry policy changes that had been made in relation to community forestry in Nepal.

Dearden and Underwood, 1998

In this section, we have looked at what we mean by curriculum development, and why participation in curriculum development is so important. We have also considered some benefits and some challenges associated with PCD.

In the next section, we look more closely at learning and consider how and why learning takes place.

Section 2: Learning, change and course design

Many books try to explain to teachers and trainers how to teach or train more effectively. These books often contain some useful ideas, methods and techniques for teachers. However, these books often miss an important point: we should be thinking about *learning* rather than about *teaching and training*. To be effective teachers and trainers, we need to have some basic ideas about what we can do to encourage learning. These ideas provide us with the basic principles for designing our course.

Let's return to the three examples of learning in the introduction (pages 2–3). Compare them with your own experience and reflect on how you have learned the important things in your life.

In Example 1, the child and the farmer learned how to behave in a certain way without consciously thinking about it. They were *motivated* to learn and participated actively in the learning process, which was a natural part of daily life.

In Example 2, the trainee carpenter had made a conscious decision to learn. His livelihood depended upon its success. This kind of skills-based coaching approach has been used for many centuries all over the world. It is probably the oldest form of organized learning. Maybe you have learned something in this way. Is this kind of approach suitable for all learning?

In Example 3, the community health workers had no say about when, where or how the training course should be carried out, nor what would be achieved as a result. Do you think that this course would have helped the health workers to change their behaviour? There are some hints about this in the story. Maybe there are some other factors that you can think of which are not mentioned. Make a list of all the issues you can think of which might have affected the outcome, and see if you can suggest some things which could have been done differently. As you continue to read this book, you should be able to suggest many ways of improving this training.

So it is clear that learning can take place in different ways. Let's look now at some ideas about how people learn.

THEORIES OF TEACHING AND LEARNING

There are many different explanations for how we learn. Many of the concepts are very abstract and complex, and there is still a lot of debate about them. Let's look at some of these theories.

▶ Some scientists believe that we can explain learning in terms of behaviour. They believe that if we provide the right conditions and stimuli (for example, facts and information linked to different kinds of reward) people will learn what we want them to. This theory has led to the idea that a teacher can transmit knowledge to learners. This is a *behaviourist* approach.

▶ Others believe that teachers first need to understand how the brain works: for example, how we perceive and memorize things, and how we process information. This enables a teacher to present information in such a way that learning will be more effective. This is a *cognitive* approach, and a lot of approaches for teaching children are based on this.

▶ Still others believe that learning is more complex. Each person has his or her own personal experiences and is part of a wider society, so all people are affected by the unique contexts in which they live. This means that each learner has a unique mental picture of reality. When new information or experiences are presented, then each learner has to relate this new information to his or her existing mental picture and construct a new map of knowledge. For example, think about how you felt before you learned to ride a bicycle. You probably thought of it as a very difficult skill. But once you learned how to do it, it seemed easy and natural. So the mental map of reality has changed. Teachers and trainers still need to think about how to structure and present information, but it is even more important to think about the experiences offered to learners. In this approach, the attitudes and beliefs of the individual become very influential on how he or she learns and how he or she behaves. This approach is usually called *constructivist*.

You can see that there is not one universal theory of teaching and learning. If there were, then life would be a lot easier!

A theory helps us predict what will happen if certain events or actions take place under certain circumstances. So, as teachers and trainers, we need to understand theories of teaching and learning. We also need to learn from our own experiences and those of other successful teachers, and develop our own theories about learning and how we can improve our teaching.

In the next few pages, you will find some basic principles and ideas to help you shape your theories of teaching and learning. Later in this book, you will find some concrete suggestions for how you can put your theory into practice.

HOW DO ADULTS LEARN?

This book is aimed mainly at teachers and trainers of adults, although teachers of children will also find many of the ideas useful. But let us concentrate on adults now.

Adult learners

► bring with them a wealth of experience.
► define their own learning needs, based on their own perception of what they need, and have a basic desire to be independent (from a trainer) in doing so.
► are self-directed.
► want to be able to position the offered knowledge and skills in the context of their experiences.
► can learn from each other's experiences, and need interactive training methods (open communication between facilitator and participant, and among the participants).
► need a safe learning environment.

We already looked at three examples of learning. Let's take one more example. Can you ride a bicycle? If so, can you remember how you learned to do it? Did you do any of the following?

► Read a book about how to ride a bicycle.
► Read a manual about how a bicycle works and how you can take it apart and repair it.
► Watch other people riding bicycles.
► Ask someone to show you how to ride a bicycle.
► Get on a bicycle yourself and asked someone to help you learn how to ride it.
► Get on a bicycle yourself and just try it out without anyone helping you.
► Go on a training course to learn how to ride bicycles.

Figure I.2.1: How did you learn to ride a bicycle?

If you did some of these things (and probably you did), in which order did you do them? Perhaps you watched others first, and then asked someone to help you. Perhaps you just tried it out yourself, fell off a few times, and eventually managed to keep going until it became easier. Once you knew how to ride a bicycle well, maybe you read a book about bicycle repair, so that you could maintain your bicycle. In some countries, many children attend short training courses to help them ride bicycles safely on roads where there is a lot of traffic. In other places, books and training courses are either not available or too expensive.

The important point from this example is that there are different ways to learn. The example of the bicycle is also nice because we often say that once you have learned to ride a bicycle, you never forget. So it shows that learning can lead to a permanent change of behaviour.

A lot of educational research has shown that there are four main steps which enable adults to learn effectively. This has been called the *experiential learning cycle*, and it is shown in Figure I.2.2. The four steps are:

▶ experience: something happens directly to the learner, maybe seeing, hearing, trying out something.
▶ reflection (questioning): the learner asks themselves or others questions about what happened during the experience.

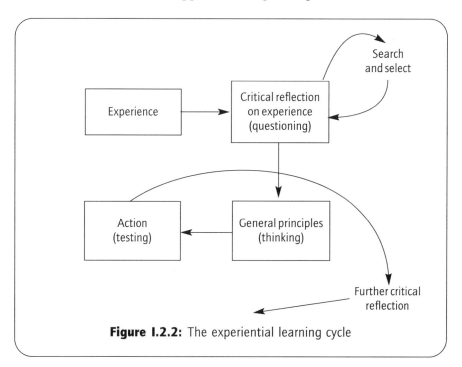

Figure I.2.2: The experiential learning cycle

▶ thought: the learner uses the answers to the questions to build up a theory based on what actually happened during the experience.

▶ action (testing): based on the theory, the learner tries something out, to test whether the outcomes of an action are as they expected.

As learners go through a continuous cycle of experience, reflection, thought and action, they start a gradual transformation. This is really what education is all about. It is not about the accumulation of facts and figures which may never be of practical use.

Education is about personal change, which can take place in different areas of our lives:

▶ cognitive change: moving from thinking in a rigid and closed way to learning as a process and thinking creatively in systems.

▶ change in behaviour and attitudes: questioning beliefs and values about the role of education and educators, about who has what knowledge, about what knowledge is of what worth, and where power is vested in society.

▶ change in emotions: building self-worth and confidence, developing personal identity and common sense, identifying what motivates each person, articulating needs and finding solutions.

A lot of education and training programmes do not enable learners to learn in these different ways. PCD aims to encourage learners to learn in all these ways. We would say that this type of learning leads to real personal development. The experiential learning cycle is a very valuable tool in helping people to learn and develop themselves effectively.

LEARNING STYLES

We will look shortly at how the experiential learning cycle helps us to design an effective training course, but first we need to consider one more important issue about learning. So far, we have talked about learners, suggesting that they are all alike. In our examples, however, we have talked about individuals: the child learning to walk, the farmer learning to harvest maize, or you learning to ride a bicycle. Teachers and trainers work with groups of people – we cannot provide a unique training course for every learner! However, it is still important to remember that each learner is an individual who prefers to learn in his or her own way.

Think again about how you learned to ride a bicycle. What did you do first? Watch someone else? Read a book? Jump on and try it out?

Everyone has a preference about how he or she learns things. Think about yourself and some people you know: do you recognize them in these descriptions?

1. Some people really like trying out new things. They are not very interested in theories. They don't mind taking risks, and really enjoy new experiences. Usually they don't need to watch someone else show how something is done, they just try it themselves. These people are the *pragmatists*.
2. Some people prefer to prepare before they act. They like to take their time and don't want to be rushed. They also often enjoy guiding and supervising people and processes. These people are the *reflectors*.
3. Other people like to understand theories and try to understand why certain things take place in particular way. They are not so interested in applying things in practice, but spend a lot of time thinking about 'what if . . .' . These people are the *theorists*.
4. Finally, some people really enjoy using things they have learned in practice. They like to apply something they have learned as quickly as possible. They love demonstrations, watching others so that they can try it out themselves. These people are the *activists*.

Most people fall into one of these four main learning styles. Let's return once more to the example of the bicycle.

▶ Did you just jump on and get going without any help or assistance from books or people? Probably you are a pragmatist.
▶ Did you start by asking yourself a lot of questions before trying to ride the bicycle, like 'Why do I really need to ride a bike?' and 'Have I done anything else like this before which I can use to help me learn?'? If so, then you are probably a reflector.
▶ Did you read a book or a manual about bicycles first? If so, then you are probably a theorist.
▶ Did you watch others riding bicycles, or ask someone to help you to get on and ride? If so, then perhaps you are an activist.

No style is better or worse than another. They are just natural tendencies which mean that most people prefer one way of learning over the others. We can of course learn to ride a bicycle using any of the above methods, but it may not feel as natural and we might not enjoy it so much. This usually means that we are less motivated and learn more slowly or not at all.

Imagine you are a pragmatist. You want to try riding the bicycle straight away. But instead, the teacher tells you that you must first read a manual on how to ride a bike and on road safety, and then you have to watch a demonstration before you can try it yourself. Probably you will become impatient, bored and discouraged, and prefer to walk instead!

So teachers and trainers need to organize learning and to present information in a variety of ways to ensure that each learner has some opportunities to learn in the way he or she most enjoys.

A participatory style helps this to become reality. Let's also look at how we can combine the tool of the experiential learning cycle with our understanding of learning styles to make learning processes more effective.

Motivation and effective learning

Using a variety of learning approaches can help learners to enjoy learning more. This is important because it helps them to keep the natural motivation which they bring to learning. A person's motivation is based on the strength of his or her desire to do something. If someone wants to do something very strongly, then we can say that he or she is motivated. You might ask yourself, 'Am I motivated to read this book?' If you have read this far, then probably the answer is 'Yes'. So why are you motivated? Finding the answer to this question will help you to understand motivation. But first, let's look at the relationship between motivation and how learning is organized.

Think back to our second learning example of the young carpenter. He learned by doing and was coached by someone who had a lot of experience. This was the most common way to learn until it was decided that children should learn special knowledge by going to school. Teachers would pass on knowledge by telling the students what they needed to learn. The learners sat and listened while their teachers taught.

This method of education is now used all over the world. Often, teachers and trainers use the same methods with adults as for young children. Many of you reading this book have probably experienced this kind of teaching. You may use this method yourself.

So what is the problem with teachers or trainers talking, and course participants listening?

Think back to the theories about learning (pages 26–7) and the four learning styles we looked at. Do they give you some clues?

This approach to teaching, when used continuously, does not work very well for children or for adults. This may surprise you, because it is widely

Stage of the experiential learning cycle	Description	Implications for teaching and learning
Experience	Learners acquire new knowledge, skills or attitudes.	Learners engage with a new situation. This can be provided through a formal teaching session (lecture, presentation, demonstration, film, computer-generated activity), through participatory learning methods (role-play, games, simulations), by field trips, visits, etc. These kinds of activities appeal especially to learners with a pragmatist learning style.
Critical reflection on experience (questioning)	Learners process the information by reflecting on the experience. This stage may also involve the learner actively *searching out and selecting* additional information to support the experience.	Learners reflect through individual exercises, group discussions, case study analysis, etc. These kinds of activities appeal especially to learners with a reflective learning style.
Thought (general principles)	Learners think about how their new knowledge and skills relate to their own context and situation, and how they can be applied in other situations.	Learners structure and verbalize their new knowledge, and answer questions such as 'What does this knowledge mean to you?', 'How will it affect your performance?', 'How will you apply it and in what way?', 'What do you feel about this learning?', 'How have your values changed?' These kinds of activities appeal especially to learners with a theorizing learning style.
Action (testing/doing)	Learners apply what they have learned in the real context – this becomes a new experience and the cycle again continues with further reflection, generalization and action.	Learners try out new skills, or attempt to solve real problems with their newly-developed knowledge, for example through field work, practical exercises, etc. These kinds of activities appeal especially to learners with an activist learning style.

used. But it is widely used for one main reason: most teachers and trainers use the same methods which they experienced when they were learners.

Let's consider some of the reasons why we say it does not work well. Look at the following picture.

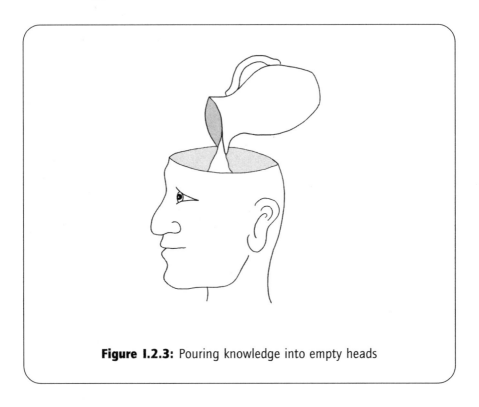

Figure I.2.3: Pouring knowledge into empty heads

Often when people see this picture, they notice several things. First, they say that the picture shows the head of the person is empty. Second, they often suggest that the content of the jug is knowledge. You might think of some more questions about the picture, such as:

▶ What is inside the head of the learner? Is it really empty?
▶ Can knowledge be poured (or transferred) from one place to another?
▶ Who is holding the jug of knowledge?

This way of teaching and learning encourages learners to memorize facts and information. The famous educator Paulo Freire called this approach the 'banking' of knowledge: storing knowledge in the minds of learners for the future.

Unfortunately, this type of learning is short-lived. Learners memorize information without understanding it. This means they do not remember it for long and they cannot use it in their daily lives.

When this method is used, children and adults may seem not to be interested or motivated, or to be lazy. But are they to blame? Remember what we said about preferred learning styles. A common question by teachers and trainers is 'How can we motivate our learners?' Increasingly, educators are realizing that motivation has to come from the learners themselves.

Think back to the first learning example of the child learning to talk or the farmer learning when maize is ripe. They did not need to be motivated by a trainer. They motivated themselves.

If motivation helps learning, then it will not surprise you to learn that lack of motivation blocks learning. A key role of a teacher or trainer is to find out what motivates their learners. They must then organize the training course to help the learners achieve the goals they have set for themselves.

Let us think for a moment about how we deal with the behaviour of our learners. There are two strategies used very commonly by teachers and trainers: giving punishments and giving rewards.

Punishments

It is common in many school classrooms for students to be beaten for being late or for not doing an assignment. In one school, the headteacher beat the teachers if they were late coming to school! Adult learners are not usually punished physically, but they may be insulted or made to feel that they are inadequate, ashamed or guilty.

Hopefully it will not surprise you that punishment does not motivate learners and it does not lead to learning. Punishment encourages learners to behave in ways to avoid the punishment, which is not the same thing as getting them to learn something. A punishment may make students change their behaviour, to sit quietly and give the appearance of listening, but you cannot force them to learn. Only they can learn for themselves.

Punishment is also about the power of the teacher or trainer to control the learner, to say that someone has 'failed'. It is not about learning. From a wider social perspective, there is very strong evidence that people who are punished often go on to punish and oppress others themselves. Real participation changes the balance of power so that learners' and teachers' rights and aspirations are respected and used as a basis for dialogue. Punishment does not fit with this kind of approach.

Rewards

Many teachers and trainers do not use punishments and that is a good thing. But it may surprise you to read that rewards also do not motivate learners to learn effectively. You may well think, 'What's wrong with rewards, like small presents or gold stars?' Most teachers and trainers use rewards and most people like receiving them. Usually, we see desirable behaviour when rewards are on offer. But, as with punishment, the behaviour is not directed towards learning. It is only intended to gain the reward.

Some years ago, a researcher tested this idea. Two groups of students were asked to carry out a task which they enjoyed. After some time, the researcher gave one group of students a small financial reward for doing the task. What was the result? The group which received the reward lost interest in the task itself and only carried it out to gain the reward. The group which received no reward continued to carry out the task with evident enjoyment. Many experiments in different places confirmed this.

If you only want people to carry out a mechanical or physical task with tangible results, such as collecting firewood, then you may not care whether or not they are interested in the task. So you can give them the reward, and as long as they collect firewood, that is fine, even if they do not enjoy it.

However, learning is different. Real learning happens inside the learners. The content of what you learn is important, so you cannot pretend to learn. There is a simple lesson for teachers and trainers in this. We need to find out what motivates learners to actually learn. Rewards simply confuse the learner about why and what they want to learn, so it is best to avoid using them.

These ideas give some hints about the approaches a teacher or trainer should use in order to help learners learn effectively. These approaches are not easy, especially for teachers and trainers who have never experienced them themselves. Figure I.2.4 shows some practical tips to help you apply them.

Create a suitable environment for learning
Stimulate interest
Agree on why learning is needed
Link new learning to previous learning
Be clear when giving explanations, directions, etc.

Be enthusiastic
Provide structure
Set manageable and achievable tasks
Avoid being critical

Agree on clear goals
Clarify aims and learning outcomes
Change the aims and learning outcomes as and when
necessary, in agreement with the learners

Provide a relevant experience
Present relevant information
Organize a relevant activity

Help learners to reflect on the experience
Encourage and guide discussion
Ask questions as needed

Help learners to link the experience to their existing
learning
Help participants to ask themselves questions
Help learners to see what they need to learn
Help learners to see patterns in what they are learning

Provide opportunities for testing and action
Learners plan how to use what they learned
Learners apply what they learned in a real situation
Close the session effectively
Make a summary
Link learning to the goals
Link learning to future activities
Help learners to feel satisfied

Figure I.2.4: Tips for teaching methods which help learners learn

LEARNING AND CHANGE

As we have seen, change in behaviour is an indication that learning has taken place: for example, in the learning examples, the child learned how to walk, the young man learned to carry out carpentry tasks.

But bringing about change is not easy. Here is an example where the learners themselves found it difficult to change.

Making the move: participatory curriculum development in Danish forestry education

When lecturers in a Danish university wanted to integrate the concept of sustainability into their forest management courses, they used a PCD workshop to enable the students to participate in the planning and development phase of the curriculum development cycle. They found that although they could see the need for change in the curriculum, the students did not.

Because students normally only evaluated courses at the end, the idea of having an input into course design was a totally new concept. The students needed to be more empowered, because in a university the lecturers are in a very powerful position. These power relations have to be recognized and changed in order for effective participation to happen. One workshop was not enough to help the stakeholders (in this case the students) go through this change process.

This is where experiential learning is important:

Experiential learning theory has shown us the importance and role of real-life experiences in the learning process. Incorporating experiences, which highlight the need for change towards sustainability in forest management, seems to be the most important activity for faculty to engage in, in order to establish a common platform of understanding.

(Leth, Hjortso and Sriskandarajah, 2002)

Obviously, PCD poses challenges for teachers and learners alike. Teachers and trainers need to reflect and re-examine their roles, and the power which they hold. Here is an example of a strategy where curriculum change is being brought about in a participatory way, by empowering teachers to become reflective learners.

PCD in a Hungarian agricultural university

In Hungary in the 1990s, university teaching programmes in agriculture were oriented toward a state-run, centrally-planned economy. University curricula and lecturers' skills had to be transformed to meet the needs of an increasingly market-led economy, but it was difficult for the lecturers to see how they could change their teaching and learning programmes.

In cooperation with two universities in western Europe, they started with one subject of the agriculture degree programme. The first step was to create a critical mass of teachers in the faculty who had undergone training and who could lead the curriculum development process. Teachers were selected for their enthusiasm and willingness to learn as well as their teaching skills. They travelled to experience different ways of teaching and learning as well as different approaches to agricultural production. The leader of the university faculty was a real 'champion of change'. The critical factors in the change were good leadership and the will to change.

After two years of the project, the momentum for change was so great in the university that a much wider process of curriculum revision began, and almost all teachers wanted to participate to avoid being left behind by the growing movement for change. A dynamic process was initiated, which went far beyond the expectations of the project.

(Van den Bor, Wallace, Nagy and Garforth, 1995)

SUMMARY OF PART I

In Part I, we have been thinking about participation, what it means, and why we should follow a participatory approach to education and training. We looked at who should participate, and why, what participation means in practice, some challenges for PCD and how you might overcome them. We also introduced a curriculum development cycle which can be followed as a basis for PCD. We considered how and why learning takes place and looked at different learning styles. We then considered motivation and identified different factors that can block effective learning, as well as some strategies and methods you can use to facilitate learning in a participatory way.

Before moving to the next part of the book, do reflect on what you have read in the previous pages. Think about your own experiences of teaching and learning:

▶ How do these issues and ideas relate to your experience?

▶ What problems and challenges have you and your colleagues faced?

▶ What strategies have you used to deal with them?

▶ What processes or methods have you monitored and how?

▶ What has worked well and what not so well?

▶ Which of the ideas in this section might help you overcome your challenges?

These are just a few of the questions you might ask yourself, or, even better, find time to sit down with your colleagues and discuss. It is worth prioritizing some time to do this. Your work, and your own learning, will benefit as a result.

After asking the questions, what next? Is there room or a need for change? How could this change be made to happen? You may come up with a theory, you might predict that if you do x, then y will result. But how will you know if your theory is correct? Well, of course you have to try it out. This will become your new experience for your next round of experiential learning.

PCD is not easy, but many people involved in education and training all over the world are finding ways to make things happen. Part II of this book will help you follow the different phases of the PCD cycle and translate them into a process of training course design. You will discover that you can follow these phases for the design of other learning experiences, such as workshops or seminars. You will also find this relevant when you look at lesson planning, on pages 112–13. So now, read on to Part II, and find out how to put PCD into action.

Part II
Making it work –
PCD in action

Introduction to Part II

In Part I we looked at some of the basic concepts, principles and theories which are important in participatory curriculum development, teaching and learning. Many of the ideas are rather abstract and in Part II, we aim to show how you can put PCD into practice. When you apply these methods and approaches, the theories we have discussed should acquire new meaning. Please refer back to Part I as you try out ideas in this part, to help you construct your understanding of participatory curriculum development.

In the remainder of this book, you will find a lot of practical ideas which have all been tried and tested in many different settings, so we know that they do work. Very often, they have been adapted and changed to suit the context, the particular sector, or the participants involved. Try to adapt them for your context. There is no correct way to use PCD, but try to use the principles and theories in Part I to guide your work.

The framework for Part II is provided by the PCD cycle on page 23. This will guide us through the PCD process.

You will remember that there are five main phases in the cycle. At the centre of the cycle is stakeholder involvement. This is to show that stakeholder involvement is not a separate phase. It is a key element of every phase and it is the means by which curriculum development becomes a participatory process. Finding out how to work with other stakeholders is a challenge which you will need to take up if you intend to follow a PCD approach.

1 / Situation analysis/ training needs analysis

RAISING AWARENESS

How do you get started with PCD? A good first step is to organize a workshop for the group of people who will be mainly involved in designing the training course. We are going to focus quite intensively on this workshop, because it is a critical event in the PCD process.

This group will probably include you and some other colleagues who are directly involved in the training process (for example, other teachers, or managers with a responsibility for course design or for running the training course).

If you have read Part I, you should now be aware of some ideas which may be new to your colleagues. This is why you are organizing an awareness-raising workshop! Try to involve the participants in the planning of the workshop before it begins, and by providing relevant information in advance. It is important to develop a common understanding among everyone who will be involved closely in the curriculum development process. Raising awareness of PCD and its principles at a workshop gives you and your colleagues an opportunity to clarify and agree goals, aims and some basic principles.

It is important to plan and organize the workshop well, otherwise there may be a lot of discussion which does not move things forward or is on unrelated topics. However, do not expect everyone to agree on all the issues. This is rarely possible and it also is not very helpful. Different views and opinions can help to see the issues in a new light, so they are a vital part of development. What is important is to find a way to use all the ideas constructively.

Here are some suggestions for organizing a workshop which will help you raise awareness of your colleagues and gain a common understanding.

PREPARING A WORKSHOP FOR PCD AWARENESS-RAISING

There are different types of workshop. Some workshops are very structured, with a detailed programme planned in advance. This is important if you intend to use the workshop to present information. Good planning will ensure that you have enough time for presentations and discussions. You may also want to follow a specific process with particular steps. But workshops can also be more flexible. You can plan an outline of a schedule, but agree the details with the other participants at the start of the workshop. Then you can be more responsive to issues which emerge. It is a good idea to build in some flexibility when you plan a workshop.

Here are some tips:

▶ Decide on a suitable time for the workshop. Try to find a time when everyone is not under high pressure. You should plan two to three days for an awareness-raising workshop.

▶ Choose a suitable location for the workshop. It is often a good idea to hold it away from your normal workplace, otherwise it is easy to become distracted and drawn into your usual workload. Also, going to another venue is a good way of bonding colleagues in a mutual experience.

▶ Make a draft programme and circulate it to other participants as early as possible and ask for their feedback. Make changes if necessary. If you send a draft programme out for comments the day before the workshop, it sends the message that you are not really interested in the input of other people. This would be a big problem if you are really committed to a PCD approach. The draft programme may contain the following elements:
   • a short explanation of why this workshop is being organized
   • aim of the workshop
   • expected outcomes
   • names of the participants
   • logistics, such as location, timing, etc.
   • outline of the programme.

The workshop methodology and process will depend partly on the aim of the workshop and the expected outcomes, but also on how participatory you want to be. Some workshops are very top-down, whereas in others people feel very involved and that their voices are heard. There is a trade-off, of course. If there is an opportunity for everyone to speak and get involved, this will take more time. You need good management and planning to set up a process which is very participatory yet still ensures that the aims are achieved.

Identifying the process gets easier with practice, and an example is given below to help you. Here are some of the things you need to think about:

▶ Consider factors such as the number of participants, the location (indoors/outdoors, large or small room, fixed furniture or moveable chairs and tables) and the cultural context.

▶ Be aware that many people are not accustomed to participatory methods in a workshop. Some people may not feel comfortable about taking part in activities or in role-play, singing or acting.

▶ Start with activities which you feel will not be too threatening for participants unfamiliar with participatory workshops. If they react well, you can be more daring!

▶ Be prepared for some resistance. Sometimes, participants may appear not to understand instructions, or they ask a lot of questions to avoid starting the activity. Sometimes, you may just have to insist that everyone starts the activity: usually the outcome is not nearly as bad as people expected!

▶ Delaying tactics may indicate insecurity over a particular topic or subject, rather than over the method. Give people a chance to discuss their fears or concerns.

▶ Remember that most people do prefer to be actively involved rather than passively sitting and listening to others.

Here is an example of a programme for a PCD awareness-raising workshop.

Example: Participatory curriculum development workshop, forestry college, China

Day	am	pm
1	Welcome and introductions Expectations of participants Organization of daily feedback sessions (1 hour) **Key question 1: What is our concept of curriculum development for the college?** Brainstorming in groups: • what is involved in curriculum development? • who is involved in curriculum development? Feedback and discussion (1 hour)	Warm-up (10 minutes) **Key question 3: What is PCD?** Overview of the PCD process (presentation): • concepts of CD • models of CD • stakeholders and the PCD process • the PCD cycle. Plenary discussion (clarification of points) (1 hour) **Key question 4: Has PCD been tried anywhere else?**

Day	am	pm
	Key question 2: What do we hope to achieve through curriculum development? Forcefield analysis • group exercise Discussion (1 hour)	Presentation of case study from Vietnam (1 hour) **Key question 5: How does this approach relate to what we have learned and done already?** Discussion on links with earlier learning on training design and stakeholder participation (1 hour)
2	Review of previous day's learning (15 minutes) **Key question 6: How do we carry out a stakeholder analysis in PCD?** Stakeholder analysis for PCD: concept and methodology Presentation (30 minutes) **Key question 7: Who are the stakeholders?** Group exercise on stakeholder identification: • group exercise • feedback session (1 hour) **Key question 8: How are the stakeholders related and what are their interests?** Stakeholder mapping of relationships and conflicts • Group exercise (1 hour)	Warm-up (10 minutes) • Feedback session (1 hour) **Key question 9: How can we involve the stakeholders?** Drawing up a full stakeholder matrix • group exercise • feedback session (2 hours)
3	Review of previous day's learning (15 minutes) **Key question 10: How do we move forward from here?** Stakeholder participation matrix – review, discussion and revision (45 minutes) Prepare draft proposal for PCD at the Forestry College • group exercise • feedback session (2 hours)	Warm-up (10 minutes) Prepare rough action plan and budget estimate • group exercise • feedback session (1 hour) Final presentation of outcomes to key persons of the forestry college, discussion, review. (1.5 hours) Workshop evaluation (30 minutes) Close of workshop

RUNNING THE WORKSHOP

In PCD events, as in all participatory activities, good facilitation is needed. This may be done by you, by one of your colleagues or by someone brought in from outside. If the workshop is small and you think it is unlikely that a lot of disagreement will occur, then you can probably facilitate it yourself. If, however, you expect a lot of disagreement or if you want to be really involved in the discussions yourself, you may think of asking someone else to facilitate the workshop. This has the advantage that the facilitator can concentrate on running the workshop and you can take part. The drawbacks are that an outside facilitator will require a fee and it is important to find someone with good skills. Some points about facilitation skills are mentioned on pages 104–5.

Introducing the workshop

Many workshops begin with an official opening, although it is not necessary to have one. Sometimes these are needed for reasons of protocol, and they can be encouraging for participants if a few well-chosen words are said by someone who can say them in a relevant and interesting way. But it is important to stress that the time for this part of the event will be limited. You should also aim to start the workshop on time, and if a guest of honour is late, it may be possible to begin the programme and still allow the guest to fulfil his or her duty on arrival. Time management is important in every workshop, and all participants should appreciate this fact from the beginning.

The first activity of a workshop is almost always introduction of the participants. There are many ways to make this a useful, interesting exercise and also to limit the time it takes.

Here are some ideas for ice-breakers. These are short, focused activities which help people to get to know each other and gain confidence in the group.

- Give all participants a piece of card. Ask them to fold it lengthwise and to write their name on it clearly. They can keep this in front of them throughout the workshop so that their name is visible to everyone. Or you can give everyone a small circle of card and a pin, and participants can make a name badge to wear during the workshop.
- Give clear instructions on how each person should introduce him- or herself. For example, to say his or her name and one sentence on his or her institu-

tion, one sentence to describe his or her job or responsibility, and maybe one thing he or she hopes to learn at the workshop. Or you can give a maximum time limit, for example, 30 seconds.

- Ask each person to think of something more personal to include in his or her introduction. For example, he or she could mention:
  - something nice which happened to him or her in the last year
  - something (a person or event) which has influenced him or her strongly
  - something important he or she intends to do in the near future.
- Ask participants to sit side by side in pairs and to interview each other for 3 minutes. Each participant then introduces his or her partner.
- Ask each participant to find one person in the room he or she does not know, interview him or her and then introduce him or her to the group.
- Introductions can also be done in a more visual way. For example, ask participants to draw a picture which describes themselves on a large piece of paper. You can structure this by suggesting some key headings for parts of the picture, such as 'my work', 'my interests', 'my strengths and weaknesses' or 'my hopes and fears'. The pictures can then be put up on the wall like an art gallery and everyone can look at the pictures and ask questions.
- If it is a really imaginative and lively group, ask each participant to act out something which reflects his or her personality, such as an animal, bird, or some other object. The other participants can then try to guess what each is acting, and the person can explain why he or she chose that image.
- At the end of the introductions, another nice ice-breaker is to ask each person to shake hands with every single person in the room – no one should miss out anyone! This makes everyone very active, and brings everyone into contact as well.

The next step is to find out what participants expect from the workshop. Every participant at a workshop has some expectations. Some people may have very specific expectations, others may be rather general. The case study in the box below shows why it is helpful to find out what people expect.

A true story about expectations

At the beginning of a PCD awareness-raising workshop, the facilitator asked the participants why they had come to the workshop. Different participants gave various answers. One participant then said, 'I have come to learn how to vaccinate pigs.' This was rather surprising, because the workshop was about

PCD. It was then discovered that the participant was an animal health adviser, but he had come one week early, and was indeed expecting to learn about pig health. Once he realized his mistake, and after a few moments of embarrassment, he became quite cheerful and said, 'It does not matter. Education is also very important and I would like to stay and learn about curriculum development. Besides, I came a very long way to attend this workshop, and now I should make the most of my opportunity.'

He went on to be an excellent participant!

It is good to discuss expectations before you introduce the programme, so that you do not influence people too much. Ask participants 'What are your expectations from this workshop?', and give them five minutes or so to reflect quietly before they respond. They can give their responses in different ways.

- Ask participants to include their expectations in their personal introductions
- Ask each individual to write his or her expectations on small cards (one expectation on each card, in nice large writing). These can be collected and posted on a flipchart, and then sorted into categories (see group exercises in the methods section for more detail on how to do this, on page 127).
- Ask participants to discuss their expectations in a group. You can use the merry-go-round exercise (see pages 124–5), the snowball exercise (pages 123–4), brainstorming (pages 121–2) or the fishbowl (pages 125–7).

Keep the expectations somewhere visible: for example, pin them on the wall, so you can all refer back to them as a checklist for progress. They will also be useful at the end of workshop evaluation, so that participants can see if their expectations have been achieved.

Hopes and fears

Another useful exercise for the workshop introduction is 'hopes and fears'. When a group is working together for the first time, or tackling a new or difficult activity with a new approach, some people may feel hopeful about what they can achieve, although they may also have some fears. For example, they may fear disagreement in the group, or that the workshop will not achieve what they expect. Sometimes, it is helpful to give people the chance to say what their hopes and fears are. This can be done through brainstorming, or through a group exercise with a written output, or even by making a picture or acting. Once the hopes and fears have been identified, participants may feel more open about discussing things in general.

Also, you may be able to agree on some strategies in the group to avoid fears becoming reality, for example:

▶ participants should not come late
▶ participants should not dominate discussions (if someone is speaking too long, other participants can stand up or clap to indicate this)
▶ if anyone feels sleepy, he or she can stand up, and then everyone also has to stand up and stretch (this gives the participants a sense of empowerment).
▶ participants should switch off their mobile phones for the whole session (this is increasingly a disturbing factor in many workshops!).

If there are a lot of fears about factors outside the workshop (problems at home or work), here is an exercise which can help participants to put those worries aside until the workshop is over.

▶ Place a large cardboard box in the centre of the room.
▶ Ask each person to write down his or her fears on a piece of paper, and to put the paper in the box without showing it to anyone.
▶ Close the box, and put it away somewhere, with the comment that participants do not have to think about these fears for the rest of the workshop.
▶ If you are in an open space (and there is no risk of starting a major fire) you can even burn the box of fears, so that you can actually see your fears going up in smoke!

Figure II.1.1: Burning the fears

You can now briefly present the workshop programme. Encourage participants to compare the proposed programme with their expectations. If they match well, then you can proceed. If there are major gaps between the expectations and the programme, however, you may need to discuss whether these can be resolved. You can explain that the content should become clear as you progress through the programme. You can ask if the participants are willing to make a start and to monitor their own understanding as they go, with the agreement that they can ask questions if they are confused or having difficulties.

Sometimes, small changes to the programme will accommodate particular concerns of some participants. But avoid making major changes or promises that you cannot fulfil. Sometimes, you may need to organize another workshop in order to provide what participants are looking for. You cannot achieve everything in one workshop!

Finally, it is a good idea at this point to discuss workshop logistics, such as timing, tasks and allowances. Here are some points you might address at this stage:

▶ Agree on timing for each day (starting and finishing times, timings of tea-breaks and lunch).
▶ Agree on who has responsibility for keeping the room tidy or organized. You can introduce a rota system so that a small group makes the room tidy at the end of each session or day.
▶ Agree on how you will feed back during the workshop. This is a way of reminding everyone what has happened, and it is also an opportunity to raise problems or successes. Make a chart like the one below, and ask everyone to write his or her name in a column. Aim to have the names evenly distributed. Then ask each group of people to feed back about what happened during the day.

Day 1	Day 2	Day 3
Hassan	Krishna	Samuel
Ranjita	Celia	Grace
Robert	Mpenza	Fatima
etc.	etc.	etc.

If the participants are familiar with daily feedback sessions, they can choose how they would like to present them (talking, using a picture, performing a small play, through a song, etc.). If it is a new idea, you can ask them to concentrate on the following questions:

- What did we do in the session?
- What did we learn from the session?
- What did we like about the session?
- What would we like to change for the next session?

► You could also form a 'process group' with participants and facilitators, which could meet every evening to monitor the workshop process and propose modifications where needed. Organization of this group should be done transparently. It may be best to ask all participants to nominate members of the process group. The group's role should be explained clearly to all participants. They are not 'workshop police'.

The content of the workshop

The content of the awareness-raising workshop of course depends on the specific context of the training programmes that you want to develop (look back at the different examples of workshop programmes on pages 45–6).

However, you should aim to cover at least the following elements:

► Find out participants' experience of training and course design.
► Give participants the chance to express their vision of future training courses.
► Carry out an initial stakeholder analysis.

Let's look at some practical tools to carry out these three main elements.

Finding out participants' experience of training and course design

As we have seen in Part I of this book, curriculum development may sometimes be top-down and sometimes participatory. Usually it is somewhere in between. The teaching and learning methods used by teachers are sometimes very teacher-centred (because the teacher controls the process) or more learner-centred (where the learners are more empowered and the teacher ensures that the responsibility for learning is with the learners). We can compare these two elements of curriculum development and learning and teaching methods in order to highlight different ways of working, and also the desire of the participants to bring about change.

Matrix activity

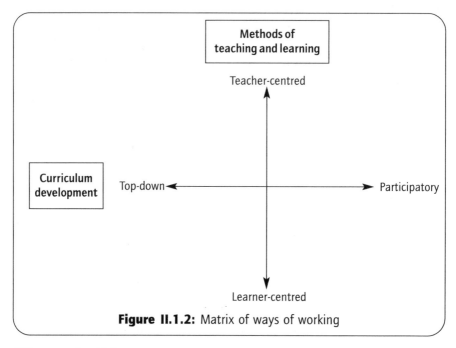

Figure II.1.2: Matrix of ways of working

What you should do:

1. Prepare a large flipchart with Figure II.1.2 clearly drawn on it and show it to all the participants.

2. Ask each participant to place a cross on the matrix which indicates his or her personal opinion about how curriculum development and teaching and learning currently takes place. If they are involved with a wide range of training courses and institutions, then they can indicate what they think is the average situation.

3. Give one or more examples, since participants may take some time to understand the matrix. Emphasize that the cross does not need mathematical precision: it should be indicative rather than exact!

4. What you should see: it is common for most participants to place crosses in the upper-left hand square of the matrix, although some marks may be found elsewhere.

5. After a short discussion about the outcome, ask each participant to come and place a circle or dot to indicate what he or she personally would like the situation to be in the future. The group should agree on a suitable future point: for example, in five years' time.

6. What you should see: it is common for most participants to place their dots in the lower-right hand square, although again you may see some variation.

7. Debriefing. Ask participants to compare the patterns of crosses and dots (present and future situations). Is this is a realistic view or an idealistic view? If there is general agreement that the completed picture suggests a change from top-down curriculum development and teacher-centred methods of teaching and learning toward more participatory curriculum development and learner-centred teaching and learning, then show this clearly on the chart.
8. Check for feedback on any marks which diverge from the majority of the responses.
9. Once you have finished this activity, display the completed chart throughout the workshop. It is very useful to refer back to, and it creates a positive attitude about change toward a more participatory approach.

This activity should take about 20 minutes. It is a plenary exercise (where everyone takes part), so try to encourage everyone to participate.

Participants' vision of future training
Curriculum development can be a long process. It is very useful to reflect on where we are now before thinking about where we are going. It is also important to reflect reality. We should not pretend that the situation is different from what it really is because we think it should be. Many people find it hard to take a critical look at their own reality. This forcefield analysis helps you and your colleagues reflect on your feelings about curriculum development.

Forcefield analysis

What you should do:
1. Make a flipchart with the following diagram on it:

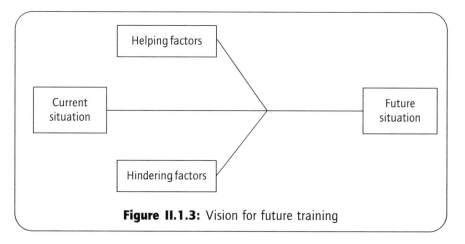

Figure II.1.3: Vision for future training

2.   Ask the participants to describe the current situation of curriculum development (maybe including strengths, weaknesses, achievements, processes) on the flipchart. Encourage them to be creative in their approach, perhaps using drawings or illustrations, or even acting out their response.

3.   The participants should then describe their vision for curriculum development for a certain point in the future. This could be in five years' time.

4.   Participants then list all the factors which will help them achieve their vision, and all the factors which are likely to hinder them in achieving it.

5.   Look at the resulting diagrams or charts. Encourage participants to compare present and future viewpoints, as well as the helping and hindering factors.

6.   Debriefing. Ask them which of these factors are most important and which cannot be overcome. Ask them to suggest ways of ensuring that a successful outcome is achieved.

7.   Display the charts throughout the workshop. They are very useful for reference, and can even be developed further if participants feel it is useful.

This activity should take about 30 minutes, including the debriefing. If you have a large number of participants, you could divide them into groups of five or six, and let each group complete the exercise and share the different results at the end. You might then need to add a little more time for the debriefing.

This activity often reveals hindering factors which people feel are very difficult to overcome. However, when they begin to discuss these difficulties together in groups, it is surprising how often solutions or options begin to emerge. During experiences of PCD, quite a number of hindering factors have emerged, but often innovative solutions have been found. Sometimes it is a question of looking for, and then opening, a window of opportunity. Here are two examples.

Problem	Solution
1. There was a lot of resistance to the idea of teachers taking responsibility for changing the curriculum. One person said 'We don't have the right to do that – only the government can make this kind of decision.' Several others agreed. The facilitator decided to let the group discuss this issue among themselves for some time.	1. A senior manager explained that teachers are free to develop detailed curricula themselves, as long as they do not change the overall balance of subjects and the names of subjects (which would require a higher level of authority). For changes within subjects, teachers could submit their ideas to the training department, and the institution could give approval.
2. A group of curriculum developers following a PCD approach had undergone a detailed consultation process with stakeholders, and had written an action plan for developing the curriculum. Then a representative from the Ministry arrived and said that the course should actually begin in the classrooms in less than a week's time. Everyone despaired.	2. Representatives from the curriculum development team spoke to the ministry representative. They knew that she had good ideas and an open mind. Once they explained the situation, and the benefits of PCD, she said to them 'But, the Minister will never find out if you do it the way you want to.' It then became clear that as long as certain things were kept rather quiet, there was much more leeway than first realized. This was one occasion when discretion proved very worthwhile!

Stakeholder analysis

You may like to look back at pages 15–17 and remind yourself of the important points about stakeholders.

One of the major activities you are likely to carry out at the beginning of the PCD cycle is the identification of stakeholders. In order to do this, you carry out a stakeholder analysis. This is a key task for you and your colleagues at the PCD awareness-raising workshop.

A stakeholder analysis identifies

▶ the key stakeholders in training course design
▶ their interests and how they are likely to affect the PCD cycle
▶ possible conflicts of interest
▶ relations between stakeholders which can be built upon
▶ the appropriate level of participation by different stakeholders at different stages of the curriculum development process.

It is good to do a stakeholder analysis early in the process of course design, so that you can involve key stakeholders from the beginning. Following the first stakeholder analysis in the awareness-raising workshop, you need to validate your results to ensure that you have identified all the stakeholders and their roles.

The best way to validate your stakeholder analysis is to organize a workshop for stakeholders, so you can gain their feedback on your analysis.

If you do not have the time or resources to do this, you can repeat the stakeholder analysis by consulting a larger group of your colleagues to validate the first analysis, or to add more information about different stakeholders. However, if at all possible, you should always try to find a way to meet stakeholders, either as a group or individually (it does not have to be at a workshop), to find out if you have assessed their roles appropriately.

Carrying out a stakeholder analysis

What you should do:

1. List the stakeholders, being as specific as possible. For example, avoid broad stakeholders, such as 'the government' or 'managers'. Be specific: 'the regional education officers', 'district hospital managers'.
2. Group them into outsiders and insiders.
3. Identify their interests in the training (expectations, benefits, resources offered or withheld).
4. Note any conflicting interests.
5. Highlight relationships between stakeholders. (Are they positive or negative?)
6. Assess the impact of developing the curriculum/providing training on the stakeholders' interests. (Will the training have a positive or a negative effect on their interests?)
7. Construct a table as shown in the following example.

Time needed: about two hours, including a plenary feedback.

Stakeholders	Interests of stakeholders	Impact of change on stakeholders' interests
a) Outsiders		
b) Insiders		

8) Analyse the relationship between different stakeholders, according to their relative importance and interest (time needed: 2 hours).
  - **Importance** indicates the priority given to satisfying stakeholders' needs and interests from being involved in PCD. In other words, how important or essential is it that these stakeholders are involved?
  - **Influence** is the power which stakeholders have over the training course design process. It is the extent to which people, groups or organizations are able to persuade or force others into making decisions and taking action.

Participants can find it difficult to understand the difference between the importance and influence of stakeholders. This may be partly due to the way the terms are translated and also because we naturally assume that influential or powerful people are automatically important. In fact, influential people may not benefit at all from the training, so they are less important. Here is a short story which can help to highlight the difference.

Importance and influence

In the village of Green Mountain, many children had recently stopped attending school because they were always ill with diarrhoea. During a participatory rural appraisal, it became clear that the problem was related to dirty water. It also became clear that a recently-opened small gold mine further up the mountain was polluting the water with the strong chemicals used to wash the gold. This gold mine belonged to a local wealthy landlord. The members of the village development committee asked the village health worker to provide information on water hygiene. This was possible because the local government had been instructed by the Ministry of Health to provide resources for hygiene courses for rural people.

Questions
Who are the stakeholders in the training and how important are they?
Answer: The training aimed to raise awareness of water hygiene among people in the village, to reduce sickness in the children. The parents are therefore very important as participants in the training if it is to be successful. The local health worker is also very important in the role of trainer. As the ultimate beneficiaries, the children would also be important, but not as important as their parents. The landlord is not an important stakeholder in this case, because she is not going to receive. The local government is not very important, because they are not the major beneficiaries of the training, although their popularity may increase if the training brings about desired changes!

Which of these stakeholders are most influential?
Answer: The parents are very influential, since their willingness to attend and support the training will have a big influence on the outcome. The children would probably have little influence, even though they are quite important. The landowner could be an influential stakeholder, however, since the ultimate goal of cleaner water would also depend on the gold mine cleaning up its activities, not only on the training. The local government would be influential, since they are providing the funding and resources for the training. The trainer would also be influential, since he or she would have a lot of control over the actual delivery of the training and its effectiveness.

Here are two methods you can use to do this importance-influence analysis:

a) Importance and influence matrix
Draw the matrix below on a large flipchart. Write on separate cards or Post-it stickers the names of the stakeholders on the list you have just made and stick the cards on the matrix according to the participants' view of each stakeholder's relative importance and influence (don't use glue, or it will be difficult to move them around). Don't worry about locating them exactly, since this is by nature a rather subjective exercise. Once all the cards are placed, have a look and, if necessary, move the cards until a consensus is reached.

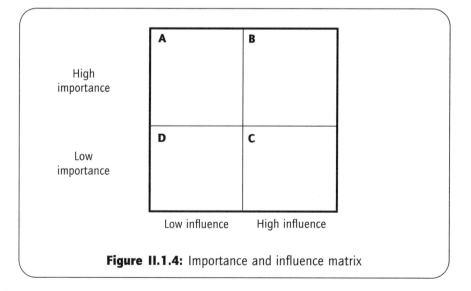

Figure II.1.4: Importance and influence matrix

How to analyse and apply the importance-influence matrix

BOX A, high importance but low influence: stakeholders placed in this box require special initiatives to protect their interests.

BOX B, high importance and high influence: stakeholders in this box require a good working relationship with the training organizers.

BOX C, low importance but high influence: stakeholders in this box may be a source of risk, and need careful monitoring and management.

BOX D, low importance and low influence: stakeholders placed in this box may have some limited involvement in evaluation but are, relatively, of low priority.

There is an example of a real matrix from a VSO curriculum developer in The Gambia on page 63.

b) Using a Venn or chapati diagram
You will need:

▶ circles made of card, in three sizes (for example 8cm, 12cm, 16cm) and in two colours
▶ triangles made of card, in three similar sizes to the circles
▶ large flipchart paper.

Take your list of stakeholders. Use one colour for outsiders and another for insiders. In the centre of the flipchart, draw a circle and write in it a title such as 'PCD' or 'training'.

Begin with the list of outsiders. For each stakeholder, decide how important his or her involvement will be and choose a circle: either of little importance (smallest circle), some importance (middle-sized circle) or great importance (largest circle). Write the name of the stakeholder in the appropriate-sized circle. Repeat for all outsiders, and then, changing the colour of the circles, follow the same procedure for all the insiders.

When every stakeholder has been written on an appropriate circle, organize and stick all the circles onto the flipchart. You can group the circles according to relationships between them: the closer the relationship, the closer the circles. You could even add lines between certain stakeholders to show formal links between them. You can add yet other dimensions, for example, frequency of involvement (the more frequent the involvement, the closer the circle to the centre of the diagram). Be aware, though, that this will quickly make the diagram quite complex.

Finally, for each stakeholder, choose a triangle (small, medium or large) depending on the degree of influence each has on the PCD process. Stick the appropriate sized triangle on the edge of the circle. Remember that stakeholders in a small circle could receive a large triangle, and vice versa. Once the diagram has been completed, take a look at it in the group, and discuss the relative importance and influence of each stakeholder until a consensus is reached.

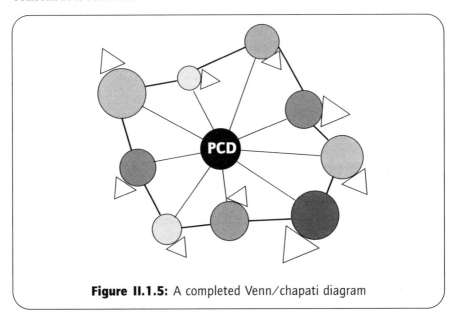

Figure II.1.5: A completed Venn/chapati diagram

For both methods (a) and (b), divide the participants into two groups who complete the exercise and then compare the results in a plenary session. The key output is not so much the finished diagrams, although they are certainly useful, but the issues that arise from the discussions. It is important to monitor progress of the groups, since some confusion and difficulties often arise during this step. Ask one member of each group to record and report back on key points arising from their group discussion.

Stakeholder analysis is rarely as simple as it seems. To get real value from it, participants should be as specific as possible and be able to justify or give reasons for their proposals. For example, if one of the stakeholders is 'the government', it is very difficult to see how 'the government' can be involved because it is too broad. Instead, participants should be specific, for example, 'the Curriculum Development Unit in the Non-formal Training division of the Ministry of Education'.

This method was used as part of a PCD cycle by a VSO curriculum developer in The Gambia. Here is what happened.

Identification of stakeholders

This exercise was conducted at the beginning of a three-week workshop to produce new textbooks and teachers' guides for Grades 1–2 in Gambian schools. I worked with a group of primary school English teachers. There was some lively discussion and participants said that they found the exercise useful. It was felt that parents, communities and regional education officers come somewhere in the middle between high and low influence. The need for employers to have a bigger input was stressed by some group members.

	Stakeholders	*Interests*
Outsiders	Parents, PTAs	Quality education
	Communities	Nation-building
	Politicians	
	Employers	Quality workers
	The Gambian nation	
	World Bank	Money well spent
	NGOs	
Insiders	Children	Quality education
	Teachers	
	Secretary of State for Education	Development of skills for workplace
	Planning Department	
	Curriculum Unit: developers	Development of personal qualities
	Inspectorate	
	Teacher trainers	Citizenship
	Regional education training	Provision of facilities and personnel
	officers	Appropriate teacher training

Relative importance and influence of stakeholders

Low influence, high importance	*High influence, high importance*
Children	Teachers
Employers	Teacher trainers
Gambian nation	Secretary of State for Education
Parents (PTAs)	Curriculum developers
Communities	Planning Department
Regional Training Officers	Inspectorate
	Regional education officers

Low influence, low importance	*High influence, low importance*
NGOs	Politicians
	World Bank

Using the output of the stakeholder analysis

As a final step of the stakeholder analysis, you can ask participants to assign potential roles and responsibilities to different stakeholders. (If you do this, then you must follow this up with the stakeholders through a participatory workshop or individual meetings to ensure that the roles they have been assigned are realistic.)

Make a table as follows:

Type of participation	Inform	Consult	Partnership	Control/decision-making
Stage in PCD cycle				
Situation and training needs analysis				
Aims				
Planning and development				
Delivery				
Develop and evaluate				

This exercise normally takes two hours to complete. Participants should continue working in the same groups as for other steps of the stakeholder analysis. If the number of participants is small enough, then each group can give a full presentation of their outputs, and everyone can discuss together. If there are more than three groups, it is better to use one of the group output sharing methods suggested in the methods section (pages 127–8).

Stakeholders may be assigned different roles because there are different levels of participation. Some stakeholders may not have time or may not want to be heavily involved in the training course design process, but they may like to be kept informed. This is a relatively low level of participation. Others, however, want to be consulted, to be asked to give advice, comments or suggestions on different aspects of the course design. It is also useful to consult certain stakeholders on aims, learning outcomes, course outlines and plans for when the training is delivered.

Some stakeholders need to participate fully in course development. The trainers and trainees are two obvious groups which need to be involved extensively, especially during delivery of the training. Other stakeholders, such as subject-matter specialists, advisers and resource persons from the community, may become real partners. Finally, for each stage of course planning, delivery and design, an individual, a group, or an institution will be in ultimate control and have the responsibility for final decisions. It is important to understand exactly who these stakeholders are in order to avoid major problems.

The level of resources will determine the extent of stakeholder involvement. Some stakeholders may need transport, accommodation, even fees, to allow them to participate. If you are organizing a PCD cycle, you do need to achieve a balance between what is ideal and what you can afford. However, if key stakeholders recognize the direct benefit from their involvement in PCD, they may be able to provide resources themselves. Discuss with potential stakeholders what may be required of them and also what they may expect to gain as a result. This is all part of a participatory approach.

The stakeholder analysis described above can help to ensure that you are well prepared as you embark on a PCD process.

Closing the workshop

Here are some points to include at the end of the awareness-raising workshop.

▶ Summarize the main points and findings from the workshop. This is most effective if participants themselves make a presentation, since it increases ownership and ensures that understanding has taken place.
▶ Check on agreement of any key outcomes.
▶ Agree on any actions needed. A simple action plan may be used for this purpose, as follows:

Action (to do)	By whom	By when	Where	Responsibility (if needed)

▶ Evaluate the workshop. (You can find tools for this on pages 138–41.)
▶ Close the workshop. Some final words may be said, and it is always good to thank the participants for their contribution and to congratulate them on what they have achieved.

Validating the stakeholder analysis: follow-up workshop

A lot of information and ideas are usually generated in the awareness-raising workshop. But not all stakeholders are represented here; it is likely to be your own close colleagues and perhaps a small number of other interested persons.

A follow-up workshop gives you an opportunity to

▶ validate main reasons and purpose of curriculum development and key areas for curriculum change
▶ discuss expected constraining and enabling factors inside and outside the institution (these two points are part of the situation analysis)
▶ introduce the concept of PCD, validate list of stakeholders in the PCD cycle and identify their roles
▶ discuss the potential for application in the institution
▶ identify organizational issues which need to be addressed for curriculum change to go ahead
▶ develop a first version of a monitoring and evaluation system for PCD
▶ validate and revise main steps for action.

Sometimes there are just not enough resources, time or money to organize a follow-up workshop. This reality faces many trainers and training institutions. In The Gambia, a VSO curriculum developer used another strategy.

Example from a VSO curriculum developer, The Gambia

It was not possible to arrange a [follow-up] workshop, but the key principles of the new curriculum were discussed on an individual level with important stakeholders. The proposed curriculum revisions were based on a nation-wide survey of teachers, parents and employers. After consultation with these key stakeholders, a detailed action plan was drawn up. Although we did not develop a monitoring and evaluation instrument at this stage, clear indicators were specified for each stage of the project. At subsequent workshops, working with groups of teachers on the preparation of materials I began the sessions with a stakeholder analysis to put things in perspective.

No situation is ever ideal, and this shows how imagination and initiative can help to overcome constraints. Awareness-raising takes time and you need to make and take opportunities whenever there is a possibility. Finding these windows of opportunity is itself an important part of a PCD process.

Now that you have done an awareness-raising workshop and a stakeholder analysis, you need to look at the wider context.

ANALYSING THE SITUATION

Before designing your training course, you need to understand the context in which the training will be carried out. This means that you will need to gather and analyse information about internal factors (such as organization of the training institution, systems and structures, existing courses, human and physical resources, etc.) and external factors (such as relevant training policies, government policies, social and economic issues, and so on).

Often, a lot of relevant information is already available from literature, previous research or community-based activities (for example, from participatory rural appraisal (PRA) or participatory learning and action (PLA) exercises which have led to the establishment of community-development plans). You can also gather useful information and ideas from key informants, such as policy-makers, field staff, experienced trainers and of course community members themselves. In addition to this, it is almost always advisable to carry out a training-needs assessment (see pages 69–84).

It is often difficult to identify all the important factors outside your training institution which have an effect on the way your institution or programme works. If you are a smaller unit or group within a larger institution, then you also need to think about the relationship with other units or departments within the overall institution. One of the best methods to do this is the Venn or chapati diagram. You already looked at one example of such a diagram (page 62). You can adapt that diagram for your situation analysis.

Another method which can shed a lot of light on an existing situation is a SWOT analysis. SWOT stands for Strengths, Weaknesses, Opportunities and Threats.

It is useful because

▶ it allows you to compare the internal situation with the external situation
▶ it is an excellent tool for encouraging a dialogue about the realities of an institution and its environment
▶ it provides a good basis for action points or strategic options.

SWOT is best used in a workshop, because a good facilitator can make a big difference between a rather superficial analysis and a really penetrating examination of a situation. SWOT does require participants to take a critical view and look at what is done well and also what is done not so well. This kind of critical analysis requires practice, and often some prompting and questioning by the facilitator.

Remember these two important rules:

▶ Strengths and weaknesses refer to the **internal** situation.
▶ Threats and opportunities refer to the **external** situation.

What you should do:

1. Divide participants into groups of no more than six. You can divide them randomly, or you can divide them according to the specific parts, units or departments of the institution from which they come. Provide each group with cards, marker pens and flipchart paper.
2. Decide on the basic question, for example *'What are the strengths and weaknesses of our institution in offering new training courses, what threats (or obstacles) do we need to overcome, what opportunities should we take advantage of?'*
3. Identify the strengths and weaknesses of the institution and write each point on a separate card.
4. Identify the threats and the opportunities arising outside the institution, and again write each point on a separate card.
5. Post the cards onto the flipchart using the matrix shown in the examples below, and discuss in plenary.

Here are the results of a SWOT analysis done by two groups in an agroforestry workshop held by the International Centre for Research in Agroforestry which examined existing agroforestry training in south-east Asia. It is interesting to note the different perspectives of the participants. A great advantage of PCD is that it allows such multiple perspectives to be seen and recognized.

a) SWOT analysis carried out by a group of extension workers and NGO staff.

Strength	Weakness

• Technology in agroforestry available
• Good training facilities:
  • demonstration farms
  • training centres
• Trainers/resources persons available with appropriate technical expertise.
	• Training material of poor quality and insufficient quantity
	• Limited skills and knowledge of training methodology by trainers
	• Not enough money/resources (not sustainable)
	• Inappropriate curricula
	• Inappropriate training needs assessment procedures
	• Evaluation systems after the training not developed
	• Heterogeneity of farmers makes training difficult

Opportunity	Threat
• Policy support from government exists • Collaboration between agroforestry institutions is high • More farmers need to be trained	• Economic crisis • Natural disasters • Unstable political condition (peace/war) • Land tenure problems

b) SWOT analysis carried out by staff of research organizations

Strength	Weakness
• Good human resources available • Potential of agroforestry system for productivity • Multi-disciplinary research teams	• Top-down approach • Coverage area too big • Gap between research and field application • Still using old-fashioned training materials

Opportunity	Threat
• New focus on community participation • Availability of new training materials	• Repeating mistakes and not learning from them • Budget problem • Lack of institutional support, training possibilities

TRAINING NEEDS ASSESSMENT

What is a training needs assessment?

We have looked at ways in which you can analyse the local situation. Now we need to think about *training needs*. PCD is based upon an understanding of the *knowledge, skills, attitudes* and *beliefs* which people need to enable them to carry out specific tasks, and behave in certain ways (see the section on learning, pages 25–40). (We use the phrase *knowledge, skills, attitudes* and *beliefs* a lot in this book, so we have shortened it to KSAB.)

The design of effective training depends upon the identification of these needs and the response which can best meet them. Identification and analysis of training needs is called a training needs assessment, or TNA.

The stakeholder analysis is an important starting point, as it can help to identify the best sources of information about training needs. For example, people who already know how to perform certain tasks effectively can provide very useful information. So can the employers or managers who supervise or employ the trainees. They are aware of new developments, difficulties and constraints. And, of course, the learners themselves are key informants, since they know best what they can already achieve and what they would like to do in the future. The team designing a course can collaborate with these stakeholders to structure training effectively. They can also bring knowledge, skills and experiences which they have found valuable. After all, they are stakeholders too!

Sometimes, training needs assessments are very exact. If someone needs to learn how to vaccinate animals, for example, then there is a clear procedure. Through observation and interviews with skilled practitioners, it is relatively easy to outline the key tasks and skills as well as the knowledge and attitudes required. Or people with a detailed knowledge of a specific job can come together to create a well-defined job description with a very detailed list of the tasks and skills required. In these cases, the course designers can identify the training gap: the difference between the KSAB which the learner already has, and the KSAB required to perform the task. This is the basis or series of building blocks for the training. The information provided by key informants and stakeholders is vital. DACUM ('Doing A CurriculUM') is a popular method to identify competences required by those who need to learn how to carry out a particular set of tasks for a specific job.

Not all situations are so clear, however. Imagine a situation where a government is steering a country from a command economy to a market-oriented economy. A national extension system is being set up for agriculture. Few government employees have received training in extension methods, yet they are expected to carry out extension tasks. They have never worked directly with farmers, but now they are expected to help farmers identify solutions to their problems. Even the farmers are not sure what crops they should grow in the new market economy. How can you design training courses in these circumstances?

There are many versions of this situation in reality. In this case, you need to follow a more open-ended, flexible and dynamic process. A wider range of stakeholders needs to be involved and their contributions may vary widely. A PCD approach will be extremely useful because it will help you to establish a dialogue between trainers, learners and other stakeholders. You will also need to think about training needs at several different levels: the training needs of an organization, the training needs of a particular job, and the training needs of an individual.

How is a TNA carried out?

A first step in assessing training needs is to analyse the needs of the organizations for whom the trainees work. Second, it is useful to carry out a task field, or job analysis: careful determination of job components, identification of what is missing to perform the job to the required standards, identification of what gaps can be filled through training, and of what type of training is needed, and ultimately prioritization of training needs. Finally, wherever possible, it is valuable to assess individual training needs. This last analysis is sometimes difficult, because you may not be able to speak to the trainees before the course. It becomes a very powerful method, however, if trainees are undergoing regular training over a period of time.

This all sounds fairly simple, but TNA is quite difficult to do well. For this reason, you may find the following methodology useful. You can adapt it to suit the circumstances of any training.

Methods of needs identification – the process

i) The basics

TNA, like all participatory research, should be planned and carried out with those who have an interest in the training. This will result in greater ownership of the learning process by key stakeholders, as well as a better understanding of what the training needs are. This is why your stakeholder analysis is a vital building block for TNA.

Through discussions with stakeholders, and also by looking closely at the situation in which the training course will be developed, you should be able to identify the main need or problem to be addressed. A problem does not have to be negative. For example, a new technology could be useful for a particular group, so the problem here is how to enable the group to know how to use that technology. Based on the problem you have identified, you can design a simple research process to identify the training needs.

ii) TNA as a research process

Many basic participatory tools, such as mapping, ranking and transect walks (see suggested reading on pages 163–4) can be used in a TNA. The methods you use depend on your situation. For example, if you are trying to find out the training needs of an organization, then you need to look at the development strategy and needs of that organization. This may require some specific methods associated with organizational development. If you are looking at job needs, then you will certainly need support from people who know what the job involves.

Once you have identified the situation, develop the training needs assessment in a systematic way by setting out the key questions you need to ask in order to address the problem. One useful tool is to match the questions with the methodology, as follows:

Questions	Source of information	Methods of collection	Responsibility	Details
What tasks does the job involve?	Current postholders, their managers, the employers	Observation (shadowing)	Trainer	Set up meetings with postholders and their managers, arrange date to shadow them at work

Logistics and strategy for the TNA

Once you have decided on the key questions and methodology, think about logistical issues. For example

- ► how many interviews?
- ► where?
- ► with how many groups?
- ► by whom?
- ► how long will this take (days)?
- ► what training does the interviewer need (guidelines for consolidation, piloting with learners and revisions where necessary)?
- ► field work: timing, resources
- ► analysis (primary)
- ► workshop – consolidation
- ► how do we present results to stakeholders?

iii) Levels of training needs

Planning identification of organizational needs

There are two steps you can follow:

1. List the organizations with a stake in the training.
2. List the questions to ask them; for example, what are the critical changes affecting the work and operations of the organization? What are the relevant organizational policies? What are the organization's current strengths and weaknesses? What opportunities and threats are there?

You can present the list of organizations and appropriate questions in a table:

Organizations	Questions

Planning identification of job needs

Use a participatory methodology for this, ideally with the trainees them-selves before the training, or with other stakeholders who can provide good quality information about the professional activities of the target group.

The following steps are recommended:

▶ Identify main categories of jobs and make a list of all the tasks associ-ated with a person in that category of job.

▶ Using interviews, questionnaires or through observation of people per-forming tasks, complete this frequency/ importance/ learning difficulty table.

Task	Frequency	Importance	Learning difficulty	Total	Priority
	1. Seldom (once or twice a year) 2. Occasional (every few months) 3. Weekly or monthly 4. Daily to weekly 5. Daily	1. Very little importance 2. Moderate importance 3. Very important	Easy Moderately difficult Difficult Very difficult		

Once the table(s) have been completed, it is useful to find out what are the priority tasks. The priorities may be stated as:

▶ low
▶ medium
▶ high.

When you prioritize, it is important to question informants on their ranking choices, for example:

► High priority – Why?
► Difficult – Why?
► What would make the task easier?
► What is needed?
   • Organizational change such as resources, structure?
   • Change in task?
   • Change in individual (KSAB)?

Through consultation with representatives of the target group and other relevant stakeholders, you can now choose one of the high-priority tasks and identify the ideal KSAB required for someone to perform it.

Task	Knowledge	Skills	Attitude/beliefs

Planning identification of individual needs

Here, it is important to estimate the training needs of individuals by preparing a list of questions to ask them, such as the following:

► How long have you worked in this job?
► What tasks do you do regularly?
► What difficulties do you face when doing these tasks or your job?
► What could help you to do your job better?
► What knowledge do you need to do your job?
► What skills do you need to do your job?
► What attitudes/beliefs do you need to do your job effectively?
► Which of these KSAB do you lack now?
► What would you like to change about your job?
► What do you like most about your job?
► What do you like least?
► Do you think you are doing a good job?
► How do you know if you are doing a good job?

You can probe (why?, when?, etc.) in more detail for each of these questions if necessary (see tips on interviewing, pages 75–7).

DATA COLLECTION

Logistics

This is the point when your plans become actions. If you have planned effectively, then the data collection should go smoothly, but be prepared and expect the unexpected. You will need flexibility, commitment, energy and organization during data collection. You should also ensure that you have enough money and resources to cover what you have planned to do. For example, if you have to travel to carry out the data collection, remember to budget for travel and accommodation costs.

Think about whether you want to reimburse your informants. If your informants have to travel specifically to meet you, then you should try to ensure that expenses related to their travel are covered. You may also want to consider paying your informants for the time and information they contribute. However, bear in mind that, as participating stakeholders, your informants will benefit from the training. In this case, it may be fair to ask them to contribute their time and information without reimbursement. This is not a straightforward issue, so be prepared for discussions and to create a solution that is appropriate to your context. However, once you have decided, it is important to communicate this clearly at the beginning, so that stakeholders are clear about the financial arrangements and have realistic expectations.

Methods

Interviewing is probably the most common tool used to gather information about training needs. You will need some skills and techniques to interview effectively. Here are general points on how you can prepare for interviews.

▶ Be clear about your reasons for interviewing a person or a group. Are you finding out about their training needs, or their opinions about the needs of others?

▶ Read secondary data such as existing reports, literature and statistics to avoid gathering information that is already available.

▶ Remember that you can use the interview to check the accuracy and validity of secondary data.

▶ Remember you have to analyse the data. Try to organize your notes in a simple way so you can easily collate and analyse the information later. Use checklists or tables.

▶ Use good communication skills. For example, develop a dialogue and do not lecture, be observant, use simple language, ask only one question at a time, do not supply answers, be flexible, be polite and sensitive.

▶ Use open questions (who?, where?, what?, when?, why?, how?). Avoid too many questions starting with 'why?', as these put pressure on the informant.

▶ Use methods (especially participatory methods) which can address several questions at once. This helps to relate issues in an integrated way and can be more meaningful to respondents. It can also raise new questions that you may not have thought of.

▶ Keep an open mind. Some information may be useful later, or other training needs may emerge which you can consider in the future.

▶ Remember that the effectiveness of training depends on the infrastructure and the context. Remember to pass on information to others who need to know it, when it is appropriate to do so.

▶ Some informants do not have the answers to some questions. Identify appropriate informants for the appropriate questions.

Content of the interview

Here are some general points to remember about the interview itself.

▶ Always greet the informants politely and thank them at the end of the interview for their time and cooperation. Remember to show your appreciation for their help.

▶ Introduce yourself and explain the purpose of the interview.

▶ Start with general questions describing the current situation. This gives informants a specific context and makes it easier for them to answer.

▶ Start with broad subjects and then concentrate on more specific topics.

▶ Be specific. Try to avoid 'big' questions like 'What do you need to learn?' This type of question is very difficult to answer and it is very difficult to analyse the response.

▶ Avoid asking leading questions which influence the answer.

▶ Probe to gain a deeper understanding.

Here is a checklist of some basic information which you should offer and collect at the beginning of an interview.

i) Introducing:
    • Introduce yourself (name, position, office . . .)
    • Purpose of the interview (this needs to be written and inserted so that everyone can explain it clearly and in the same way)
    • Timing and planning

ii) Personal information about the informant:
  • Name of the informant
  • Age
  • Sex
  • Location (district, village, etc. as appropriate)

iii) Educational/professional background of the informant:
  • Work/professional experience (years/level)
  • Training courses attended
  • Qualifications

Guidelines for note-taking

▶ Only record what you *see* and *hear*.
▶ Try to use tables or checklists to make your task easier.
▶ The note-taker should concentrate *only* on this task (*for each interview, take turns asking questions and taking notes*).
▶ Quote the answers of the interviewee where possible and if interesting.
▶ Read and fill in your notes at the end of the day.

Analysis of the data collected in the TNA

Sort your data into main categories as you collect it. That way, you will not have to organize a huge amount of data at the end of the survey. You will also see important issues emerging during the survey, so that you can explore them in more detail or clarify them during the data collection.

Examples of categories into which you could insert your data are:

▶ Policy issues
▶ Tasks related to the job carried out (present and future tasks)
▶ Client organizational issues (where students will work in future), for example, strategy, aims, staff needs, job demands, etc.
▶ Training provider's organizational issues (including existing curricula, trainee characteristics, teaching and learning approaches used, etc.)
▶ Individual needs
▶ Existing knowledge, skills and attitudes/beliefs (KSAB)
▶ KSAB needed in future.

Within each of these categories there will probably be more divisions. It is best to identify these before sorting the data.

The knowledge, skills, attitudes and beliefs (KSAB) identified in the TNA data collection will form the basis of your curricula. Once you have analysed the results of your TNA, it is important to develop a training strategy. You need to prioritize which training programmes can or should be offered. Training is not the answer to every problem and you need to have clear evidence to justify the need for any training course you decide to develop. Much of the information from TNA which is about issues other than KSAB is likely to provide this evidence and is useful when you are drawing up a training strategy. It can also be useful in identifying non-training needs.

There are different ways you can present the data. One way is to draw up a table of existing and required KSAB as follows.

Target group	Existing			Future/required		
	K	S	A/B	K	S	A/B
1						
2						
3						

A VSO curriculum developer in The Gambia presented the results of a TNA in this format. This example also highlights the link between TNA and the next step: curriculum development based upon the results of the TNA.

Experience of TNA from a VSO curriculum developer, The Gambia

A [TNA] exercise was conducted with the primary school English teachers who were engaged in writing new learning materials. I devised my own way of conducting the TNA, based on the advice of my Gambian colleague, who felt that teachers here may find it difficult to admit to a need for extra training. I felt also that it was necessary to build confidence, as the teachers in the group had no prior experience of writing learning materials.

First session

The teachers were already familiar with the principles of the new syllabus, as they had participated in the syllabus-development workshops. We began with pair discussion of existing knowledge and skills, which produced the following list.

- Subject knowledge: teachers' proficiency in English language
- How to plan lessons
- How to manage time
- Classroom management: planning a variety of different activities
- Knowledge of children: age group, ability, etc.
- Understanding of concept of learner-centred approach
- Producing their own learning materials
- Skill development
- Teaching children to understand and speak English
- Teaching children to read
- Teaching writing skills: writing legibly
  vocabulary
  spelling
  sentence structure
  grammar

Teachers in the group felt confident in these skills. As a further confidence-building exercise, we worked out the combined teaching experience of the whole group, which came to 153 years!

The teachers . . . were familiar with the concept of the learner-centred approach but did not have much experience in implementing it. The responses indicated an emphasis on writing and on the formal aspects of language learning. It was evident that [teachers] would need a crash course in child-centred, interactive methodology before [they could begin writing] the new materials.

Second session

We discussed how the teachers' existing knowledge and skills could be developed to enable them to undertake the exercise. Two areas of priority [of required knowledge and skills] emerged:

- how to develop a thematic approach in the context of language learning
- how to use child-centred methods in teaching language.

The key areas outlined below were identified and we tried to come up with some group suggestions.

Thematic approach:
- Key themes or topics at this level were identified: family, home, school, community, leisure, animals, farming, shops and markets, festivals
- How to link different language activities to topics
- How to make links with other subjects (science, and social and environmental studies).

Child-centred methods:
- Discussion of how to involve children actively
- Classroom organization: groups, pairs, etc.
- How to encourage children to ask as well as respond to questions
- How to relate topics to children's own lives and interests
- Developing confidence through achievement and positive rewards
- Getting children to take greater responsibility for their own learning.

Another way of reporting the data and results is to use the TNA to develop a competence profile. Competence profiling leads to a clear statement of what the trainees should be able to do after completing a training course. It is a very useful approach for both skills-based professional training and for more theoretical training because it focuses on application, not on remembering.

One danger of the competence approach is that it can lead to long lists of tasks which cannot be met in the time and with the resources available. You can avoid this by using the theoretical framework presented above to analyse the type of learning needed in order for a person to undergo cognitive and emotional change as well as achieving change in KSAB. This will help to focus upon the essential competences.

For example, if a community organizer wants to learn about participation, the theories and principles of participation will help the training course designers to identify the key competences which the community organizer needs in order to work effectively. Who will identify these principles? Who will ensure that the training is not over-simplified and superficial, or even counter-productive? Involve key stakeholders in finding the answers to these questions during the TNA data collection.

TNA and establishing a competence-based job profile for a farmer, Kyrgyzstan

Because of the political and economic changes in Kyrgyzstan since 1990, it became clear that the system of agricultural education needed far-reaching reform. The system of education in the Soviet era prepared agricultural specialists in any specific area of agriculture that was suitable for the requirements of that context, for example, collectivized farms. But with the growth of individual land ownership and farming, there came a need for training for a new profession: a farmer profession.

In January 2001, Helvetas-Kyrgyzstan started an experimental Agricultural Vocational Education Project (AVEP) on professional training of men and women farmers in two schools in Naryn Oblast. An important first step in the project was to define the competence profile of a farmer.

A farmer needs a lot of skills, abilities and special knowledge in order to carry out the practical activities of farming. These skills and knowledge were identified to prepare a competence profile, which was the starting point for developing a curriculum for vocational training for farmers, including teaching and learning materials.

The AVEP Project Coordinator describes the steps in the process.

Competence profile identification

Why do we need a competence profile?
1. To analyse the current situation of farms in Naryn Oblast (structure, products, market, production calendar, main problems, potentials, resources).
2. To enumerate all skills and knowledge which are needed for farming in Naryn.
3. To clarify levels of education needed (farm labourer, farmer, master farmer) and skills and knowledge desirable for each level.

Where do we get information?
1. Local farmers (from small and big farms) in villages in the catchment area for the school.
2. People from different generations (old and young).
3. Male and female.

How do we gather the information?

1. Interviewing. (School working groups were trained in basic interviewing skills.)
2. Participatory rural appraisal methodology with family groups on their farms. The following exercises were used:
   - introductions
   - transect walk (around the farm, taking photos, including a photo of the family)
   - farm profile/mapping (a big sketch on paper by the family)
   - seasonal-skills profile (making a chart of who does what, when, and who needs to learn more)
   - product ranking (listed and ranked on importance to cash, and overall)
   - problem ranking (informants listed and ranked five most important problems)
   - vision (the family draws its future farm and says what will be the main products, problems solved, what is done by whom, what skills they will have).

All outputs from these exercises were discussed.

How to evaluate the results?

1. Generalize PRA results (for example, all products, problems, activities).
2. Clarify the most common results according to what men do, and what women do.
3. Classify results into groups (such as activities in livestock husbandry, plant production, handicraft, household tasks, etc.).

How to use the PRA results in the competence profile (CP)?

1. Develope a CP template according to CP objectives.
2. Each CP chapter uses information from the relevant PRA exercise.

How to get feedback from stakeholders?

1. Distribute results to all interested sides.
2. Use feedback and comments to revise CPs.

How to present and use the CP?

The CP is the goal for education and is mainly used for curriculum development for training for men and women farmers.

What does the CP look like?

Here is an example, for 'Sheep and goat husbandry' for women farmers.

For keeping sheep and goats, a woman farmer needs the following knowledge and skills:

- Biology and physiology of small horned animals (biological structure, period of sexual maturing, physiological processes: digestion, growth, ageing, etc.)
- Classification of breed (productivity, resistance to illnesses, well adapted to local conditions, etc.)
- Principles of preparation of the most commonly-used forages (concentrates, hay, silage, fodder beet, fodder additives)
- Drawing up day-time ration according to the period of development
- Vaccination and prevention
- Veterinary processing and treatment (sanitary processing against skin parasites, end parasites, processing of wounds, bathing)
- Realization of the basic measures: births (reception of births, sanitary processing, feeding the young)
- Feeding young
- Dividing to sex/age groups (female sheep, rams, young)
- Milking, shearing and combing the down (using any equipment, be able to use the technique of shearing, evaluating the wool, pressing the wool)
- Insemination (choosing a male producer)
- Sending the animals to summer pastures (equipping the place in jailoo, building yurts)
- Observation of performance (watching animals' behaviour)
- Culling the lambs (criteria of choosing productivity, visual evaluating)
- Fattening (preparing high-concentrated fodder, making the regime of feeding)
- Butchering the animals (be able to cut the body parts, defining the quality of meat, hygiene, skin processing)
- Keeping in winter time (equipping the sheds and stables)
- Defining economical efficiency (prime cost of meat, wool, down, other production (skins, humus))
- Accounting of ratios, forages, all expenses, income
- Making production plans
- Defining the strategy of development of sheep husbandry on a farm.

To see how this competence profile was turned into an actual curriculum, see pages 100–1.

Sharing the results

Give all stakeholders involved in the TNA an opportunity to give feedback on the results. You can do this at a workshop where you present the results and participants have the chance to discuss them in detail.

However, often it is not possible to invite all stakeholders to a workshop. In this case, the results of the TNA should be disseminated in another way (for example, the written report).

If you have collected data from people or groups for whom a written report is inaccessible and who cannot participate in a workshop, it is important that you provide another opportunity for feedback during the data collection itself. When you have completed the interviews, you could hold a meeting with all the interviewees and present the findings.

Once you have collated the results from the TNA, this brings us to the end of the first phase of the PCD cycle. We have considered awareness-raising, stakeholder analysis and its validation, as well as training needs assessment. This first phase is really a vital part of the PCD process, and if you have approached it thoughtfully and rigorously, you will have laid a good foundation for the next phase of the process: developing the curriculum outline.

2

Develop curriculum outlines or frameworks

Once you have started to build awareness and relationships with different stakeholders, gathered basic information on the situation within which the training is to take place, and identified the main training needs, you are at the point of turning this information into a curriculum or a training course. Now you have to think about a new set of questions:

► Who is going to be involved in this stage of the curriculum-development process?
► Is your course a stand-alone training course or is it part of a wider curriculum?
► How can you integrate and link the new curriculum with existing courses (filling gaps and avoiding overlaps)?
► What should your course framework contain or look like?
► What activities are needed to develop the curriculum framework?

INVOLVING RELEVANT STAKEHOLDERS

Hopefully, you have already identified how different stakeholders can be involved as part of the initial stakeholder analysis, or perhaps you made it more clear in a follow-up activity when you had the opportunity to meet and talk with different stakeholders.

If you have a clear definition of training needs from your TNA, then it is possible to involve stakeholders at this point of the curriculum-development process, giving them clearly-defined roles and responsibilities.

The example below shows how a university in Vietnam kept different stakeholders involved in curriculum development after the initial TNA.

Curriculum development in a forestry university, Vietnam

The University of Tay Nguyen, in the Central Highlands of Vietnam, organized a workshop to revise the curriculum of the entire forestry degree course. The university team invited a range of internal and external stakeholders such as staff of another research institution, extension workers and local farmers. The workshop process revolved around a series of key questions:

- What will be the activities of the forestry sector in the next five years?
- Whom does the forestry sector serve?
- In the existing forestry degree programme, what needs to be improved?
- How can these improvements be made?
- What should be the aim of the forestry degree programme?
- What are the necessary knowledge, skills and attitudes to be covered by the degree programme?
- Which subjects need to be improved or supplemented? What should be the balance (in terms of numbers of periods) for the subjects in the curriculum framework?
- How should these subjects be organized over the eight semesters of the teaching programme?
- What is the relationship between subjects in terms of the theory/practice balance?
- What additional subjects are needed for final-year students?

The workshop analysed and discussed the existing forestry curriculum using a range of participatory techniques and debates. Small groups addressed the key questions, and the findings were shared and discussed.

As a result of the thorough and open debate, a clear and realistic plan was made for improvement of the curriculum framework over several years. The involvement of key institutional leaders in the workshop ensured their support at critical moments of the curriculum-revision process.

(Bao Huy, 2000)

DECIDING ON THE TYPE OF COURSE

An important decision is the type of training course to be designed.

For example, is it a

▶ stand-alone training course or is it part of a wider curriculum?

▶ short course (one day, or two or three weeks duration) or a full-time course (may be one month to four years or longer)

▶ part-time or in-service course (may be any duration, but attendance for short periods, for example, one day or an evening a week, or more intensive, such as one weekend or one week each month. In-service courses are for people who are working at the same time. Normally the training relates directly to their work, and they are given permission by their employers to attend the course.)

▶ distance-learning course (any duration, but the participants do not normally come to a training venue, they learn from their home or workplace. This type of course requires special learning materials which are sent to participants by mail or by electronic means. Internet-based learning is becoming more common and accessible.)

The length of the course is only one variable. Unless it is a distance-learning course, you will also need to decide the timing, location and format of the course, and the requirements for attendance and completion.
You will need to answer the following questions:

▶ When and where will the course be organized (so that those who will benefit can gain access to it)?

▶ Is it theoretical and classroom-based or practical, experiential and involving activities outside a classroom, for example, a field trip or work experience?

▶ Does it involve working with individuals, small groups, or large plenary sessions (or all of these)?

▶ What learning methods and materials will be needed in order to deliver the course effectively?

▶ How will the course be assessed (this is discussed in detail on pages 134–52)?

▶ How will the course be accredited (who assesses its quality)?

▶ What are the requirements that participants should fulfil in order to attend the course (qualifications, experience, financial backing, etc.)?

▶ What do participants have to do in order to complete the course (assignments, products, projects, attendance)?

▶ What resources will be required in order to run the course?

Modules

Many training institutions follow a modular approach to training. As a book is divided into chapters, the training course is divided into modules, which are shorter, self-contained blocks of comparable length, structure and value. Learners can select and study those modules which meet their learning needs. For a module-based course, you need to decide on the options for how many modules can be completed, their sequence and the timing. It is important to ensure the quality of all modules, and to consider the relative value of each module as part of an overall programme of education or training.

Modules are popular because they are flexible so that learners have more choice and control over the way they learn. This means they can fit their learning around their job or other commitments.

For training providers, it enables them to manage limited resources more creatively. Instead of updating a whole course, existing modules can be revised or removed and new modules can be introduced, depending on demand from potential participants. You might even be able to share the provision of a training course with another institution, if each of your institutions is well placed to offer specific modules.

Modular training can be very effective but it needs to be managed well. A modular system of training needs to be developed through a consultative process, which can take quite a lot of time in institutional situations.

Access to training

Think very carefully about how you can make your training programme accessible to all groups and individuals who can benefit from it.

Representatives of the following groups often find it difficult to gain access to any kind of training:

▶ women, particularly those who have a heavy responsibility caring for their family
▶ people with physical disabilities (for example, impaired vision or hearing, wheelchair users)
▶ poor people who cannot afford fees
▶ people who live in remote areas and have to travel far
▶ members of ethnic, religious or social groups (including people with HIV) who are often excluded from opportunities
▶ people who are not fluent in majority languages or who are not literate
▶ children and young people, particularly girls.

An advantage of PCD is that the process of stakeholder involvement and dialogue enables representatives of these groups to have a better chance to voice their needs and find ways of achieving their goals and fulfilling their potential.

REVIEWING THE EXISTING CURRICULUM

How can you integrate and link the new curriculum or course design with other existing courses (filling gaps and avoiding overlaps)? Once you have decided on what type of course you are going to develop, you need to look carefully at other curricula or courses which are related to the one you are working on. The situation analysis should provide you with some basic information to help you.

You can also make a more detailed analysis of existing curricula or courses to ensure that your course does not overlap and to highlight the links between courses.

You can do this by asking the following questions about existing courses (and checking out the items listed after each question), perhaps as an action research project:

▶ What is the existing curriculum content (main fields of training, balance of theory and skills, compulsory versus optional elements of training, classroom versus field-based learning, final product or credits needed for learner to complete the training successfully)?

▶ What human resources are required (teachers, administrators, technical support staff, etc.)?

▶ What methods of teaching and learning are used (methods used in the classroom, methods used outside the classroom, role of learners compared to role of teachers, responsibility of learners for determining and managing their own learning)?

▶ What are the requirements for learners to enter existing courses (qual-ifications, examinations, experience, opportunities for accreditation of prior learning where non-academic experience is used as an alternative to academic qualifications)?

▶ Financial and physical resources required (funding for existing courses, financial status of other courses – lose money, make money or just break even, availability of physical resources – buildings, equipment, books, tools)?

▶ What is the policy and management environment of existing courses (decision-making processes, stakeholders' involvement, extent of participation in governance of institutions and training)?

▶ What are the links between the training institution and other institutions (partnerships, collaborations, joint training courses, sources of competition)?

Once you have identified an approach for the new training course and the course has been designed, tested and evaluated, you can make further refinements as and when they become necessary, or even introduce new courses. You can make your course design a process of continuous improvement in which regular reflection is an important part.

DESIGNING THE COURSE FRAMEWORK

The course framework gives a general overview of the training course as a guideline for all stakeholders. It links

▶ the reality of the situation and the identified training needs
▶ the course aims and the main learning outcomes and topics of the course.

The course framework does not normally show plans for each training session. Detailed lesson or session plans will be drawn up later (see pages 112–16).

The course framework is usually divided into main topics or modules, which are based on the categories of learning needs which you identified during the TNA. The framework states the aims of the course, and you may want to include the learning outcomes.

Aims and learning outcomes

Aims are general statements which summarize more detailed intentions for the future. So, for example, the general aim 'Teach trainees how to vaccinate animals' summarizes more detailed intentions such as 'Teach trainees how to fill a syringe, teach trainees how to tie the animal securely' and so on. Aims usually set out what the trainer or teacher will do to facilitate learning.

Objectives, or learning outcomes, are statements of what the learners will be able to do by the end of the course. For example, 'By the end of the course, trainees will be able to vaccinate an animal safely.'

It can be useful to break aims down into long-term, medium-term and short-term aims, but this is a matter of choice.

Do we need both aims and learning objectives?

Everyone has broad aims. On one particular day, you might set yourself the aim to finish preparing your notes for the next day's teaching session. Training courses have an overall aim which guides their direction. Setting aims also helps you to convert the large quantity of information you gathered in your situation analysis and TNA into an overall guiding statement for the training course.

However, some trainers feel that aims are too general and that learning outcomes are all that is needed. Others believe that overall aims are needed to guide the preparation of the learning outcomes, so that you need both. And still others say that if your aims are good enough, there is no need to be more specific when planning, since learning outcomes will evolve during the course to meet the needs of the trainees.

There is no correct answer to the question of whether aims are needed. Much depends on your context. If your context is objective-oriented, it may be a good idea to write both aims and very specific learning outcomes (we will look at how to do this on pages 94–101). Many institutions prefer to see clear aims and learning objectives. But if your context is more process-oriented, you may want to set aims only, and allow learning objectives to develop during the course.

Here is an example of a very broad aim, of a College of Agriculture diploma course: *to provide a comprehensive theoretical and practical education in general agriculture*.

Here is a more specific aim, of a National Certificate Course in farm management: *to consolidate the students' practical skills and to give sufficient information of the methods of analysis and planning necessary for organizing a farm business*.

Here is an overall aim from a ministry of health's curriculum which was developed with the input of a VSO trainer. It is expressed in terms of KSAB, but it is quite general and the curriculum included many sub-aims as well as very detailed learning outcomes: *to develop the skill, knowledge and attitudes of TBAs* [traditional birth attendants] *working in the villages in order to improve the maternal and child health services in Nepal*.

We will look at how to develop detailed learning outcomes in the next section.

Here are some examples of different course frameworks which you can adapt to your own situation.

1. A course framework for a short course

▶ Title of course:
▶ Aim(s):
▶ Timing:
▶ Location:
▶ Participants:
▶ Evaluation procedure:

Topic	Learning outcomes (by the end of the course, participants will be able to:)	Content	Methods	Materials	Timing	Person responsible
1	i ii iii					
2						

2. A simplified course framework

Lessons	Learning outcomes	Teaching/learning strategies and aids

3. A course framework based on experiential learning

Content	Expected knowledge and understanding	Possible learning experiences

4. A course framework with strong emphasis on logistics

Topic	Performance objectives	Notes	Hours of theory	Hours of practice

5. A more detailed course framework (this is useful for new trainers)

Topic	Learning outcomes (by the end of the course, the learners will be able to:)	Content	Trainer activity	Learner activity	Materials and resources	Hours or periods

6. A competency-oriented course framework, with some examples of performances required

Module 1: skill set (a) – engine maintenance	Comments	Level of competence		
		1	2	3
Identify type, size and reference number of engine from engine plate.				
Strip down engine including seals and bearings.				

Once you have the overall curriculum framework or outline, it is time to go into more detail, and to develop the curriculum ready for use in training.

3 / Plan and develop detailed curricula

DEVELOPING DETAILED LEARNING OUTCOMES

We have arrived at the really specific part of the curriculum development process. By this stage you and other stakeholders should have described the reality of your situation, identified the main learning needs, grouped the learning needs into categories giving a course structure, and stated the aims of the course. It is time now to think about the learning outcomes of the course.

What is an objective or learning outcome?

An objective or a learning outcome is a statement of how learners will behave or what they should be able to do after successfully completing a course or learning experience.

In other words, there should be a measurable change in behaviour.

It is a good idea to try to say in advance what outcomes we would like from training but, as we saw in Part I, it is very difficult to predict what all learners will definitely be able to do. All learning is subjective and depends upon the individual learner.

This is why it is important to the PCD cycle to involve the learners as much as possible in setting the learning outcomes. Derive the learning outcomes from the stated aims of the course. In a PCD approach, stakeholders can be involved in setting the learning outcomes, possibly in a workshop or by gaining feedback on the first draft of the learning outcomes.

How do you write learning outcomes?

There are two important areas which you need to consider when writing learning outcomes. First, write your learning outcomes according to four basic rules. Second, ensure that your learning outcomes describe all the different domains (areas) of learning which your course needs to offer the trainees.

Four basic rules for learning outcomes
Learning outcomes should:

1. be written in terms of the learner. This means that they should express what the learner will be able to do after the course or learning experience.
2. identify the desired behaviour by name and specify behaviour which can be observed. It must be possible to assess the activity in some way.
3. state the conditions or restrictions under which the desired behaviour will occur.
4. include a criterion or performance standard which the learner must achieve to be considered acceptable.

These rules are sometimes expressed by saying that learning outcomes should be SMART:

S = specific
M = measurable
A = attainable
R = realistic
T = time-bound.

Here are some examples of SMART learning outcomes from training course curricula produced by VSO trainers and their local colleagues in a range of fields and countries.

▶ By the end of the session, the learner will be able to write learning outcomes for a course in family nutrition to the required degree of specificity.
▶ At the end of the unit, the trainee nurse will be able to describe the anatomy and physiology of the four systems (locomotor, endocrine and nervous systems and special senses).
▶ At the end of the course, community-based rehabilitation workers will have the necessary knowledge and skills to set up and carry out simple physiotherapy regimes on a short-term basis, while working under the supervision of a physiotherapist.
▶ By the end of the three-day workshop, resource workers will understand basic models of behaviour change and their application to HIV and AIDS work:
    • They will be able to explain the stages involved in people changing their behaviour.
    • They will be able to identify ways in which models of behaviour change can be applied to HIV prevention activities.

- They will be able to evaluate critically the current approaches to HIV prevention and care.

You will notice that in order to achieve a learning outcome, some change in the learner's behaviour must take place, and that this behaviour change must be measurable.

This is why learning outcomes must be written carefully, using verbs that make it clear that the learner is required to *do* something which can be evaluated. Avoid verbs which make the change in behaviour difficult to evaluate. For example, it is very difficult to measure whether a learner 'knows' something, but much easier to assess whether the learner can 'explain' something.

Some useful verbs for learning outcomes	Some verbs to avoid in learning outcomes
• define • identify • recognize • list • solve • construct • state • explain • select	• know • understand • enjoy • believe • appreciate

Learning domains in learning outcomes

You also need to ensure that the learning outcomes cover all the domains or areas of learning that your trainees will need to do in order to achieve the aims of the course.

Every learning experience involves three domains of learning:

1. The cognitive domain, which emphasizes intellectual outcomes, such as knowledge and understanding.
2. The affective domain, which emphasizes feelings, such as attitudes, interest, appreciation, beliefs and values.
3. The psychomotor domain, which emphasizes motor skills, such as writing, using tools, using hands, etc.

For example, the learning outcome 'being able to plant a tree' lies primarily in the psychomotor domain, but this task also requires appropriate knowledge and attitudes so that the tree is planted in such a way that it will grow well. You need to ensure that you provide learning experiences so the learner can gain the knowledge and attitudes that enable him or her to plant a tree successfully.

Levels of learning
Within each domain of learning, educationists have identified different levels, ranging from the most simple to the most complex. Each level assumes that all those below it have been achieved. The cognitive domain has six levels:

1. knowledge
2. comprehension
3. application
4. analysis
5. synthesis
6. evaluation.

For example, in the cognitive domain, application (level 3) assumes that the learner can recall (level 1) and understand (level 2) knowledge. Each level is more challenging for learners than the one below it: it is more difficult to evaluate than it is to know something. For this reason, many trainers and teachers focus on learning outcomes for the lower levels of the domains because these are easier to achieve. It is also more difficult to ensure that learning outcomes for the affective domain have been achieved: how do you find out if a learner 'identifies with' or 'supports' something?

The most important point to remember is the first basic rule discussed above: learning outcomes should be written in terms of what the learner will be able to do after a period of learning has taken place. This requires a shift in emphasis from what the teacher or trainer will do to what the learners will be able to do. Grasping this idea is the key to writing learning outcomes.

Here are some tips to help you:

1. Identify the domain(s) and level(s) of every learning outcome.
2. Ensure that you have a balance between the domains of the learning outcomes.
3. Ensure that higher as well as lower-level learning outcomes are included in any course (where appropriate).
4. Ensure that lower-level learning outcomes have been achieved before higher levels are attempted.
5. Devise tests which are appropriate to various levels of learning outcomes.

Let us consider an example.

A TNA has identified that '*The learner should be able to "carry out a participatory rural appraisal (PRA)"*.'

Is this an acceptable learning outcome as it stands?

Let's go back to our four basic rules for writing learning outcomes.

1.   Is the learning outcome written in terms of the learner? In this case, it is.
2.   Behaviour: What should the learner be able to do? This is not so clear. Should the learner 'know how' to carry out a PRA, or be able to practise it in the classroom, or actually be able to perform a PRA in the community? Let us assume that you expect learners to perform the PRA. This is an assessable learning outcome.
3.   Setting conditions: The learning outcome needs to state clearly under what conditions the objective is to be achieved. If the learner 'should be able to carry out a PRA', how long would he or she need to complete the activity? One week? One year? Ten years? You can make this measurable by stating, 'By the end of the course, the learner should be able to carry out a PRA.' If your course is only one week long, then you may need to ask yourself if this time-frame is realistic. Think about whether your course is raising awareness and providing information, or whether it is experiential so that the learners actually apply what they are learning.
4.   Meeting criteria: Analyse the task or activity to be completed. Ask questions like: What preparation should the learner make before the activity (in this case, the PRA)? What methods should the learner use? Where should the PRA be organized? Who should be involved? What follow-up should be organized? Evidently, you have to specify the criteria to be met: for example, the PRA might be integrated into an existing extension programme, carried out in a village with not more than 50 households, in an area which includes newly allocated forestry land, and so on. Be as specific as you can.

Your final learning outcome could therefore be:

> By the end of the course, the learners will be able to carry out a PRA in collaboration with district-level extension officers in a village in North-west Province.

This example also highlights some difficulties with learning outcomes. Carrying out a PRA involves many, many sub-tasks. So it may be necessary to break down this big learning outcome task into smaller ones, and write a series of more specific learning outcomes for the smaller sub-tasks.

The only way to learn to write learning outcomes is to try it yourself. Practise writing learning outcomes for different domains of learning and different levels of learning. Always ask someone else to give you feedback or try writing them together with a colleague. This may take a bit longer, but the result will be much better than if you do it on your own.

Stakeholder involvement is crucial throughout the PCD process. Sometimes it is hard to see how stakeholders (other than trainers or a small curriculum development group) can participate in the preparation of learning outcomes. Here is an example of how it can be done.

Stakeholder involvement in setting learning objectives in PCD, Eastern Caribbean Institute for Agriculture and Forestry in Trinidad and Tobago

The overall learning objectives were seen as the results intended from the educational programme and were derived from the occupational profile. The drafted learning objectives in knowledge, skills and attitudes for each different subject discipline matter were modified during the consultation workshop. This resulted in a stakeholders' approved list of learning objectives for every subject discipline.

Anita Hermsen, FAO (2000)

Establishing a process such as this can be difficult and time-consuming, but stakeholders will feel greater ownership if they are involved in the development of the detailed curriculum. This should lead to more effective training.

Here are two more examples of the process of establishing the detailed curriculum framework.

Establishing the curriculum framework for Gambian schools, VSO curriculum developer, The Gambia

A general outline [of the curriculum framework] was developed within the curriculum unit through a departmental workshop. This structure was discussed individually with key stakeholders. It would have been more effective to have held a stakeholders' workshop, but this was not possible. Panels of serving teachers worked to develop new syllabuses for each of the core subjects. These were based on drafts drawn up by the curriculum unit, as it was felt that the teachers lacked the time and expertise to produce the whole lot from scratch. The syllabuses contained specific learning outcomes and suggested ways of assessing and evaluating pupils' attainment. Then, the teachers were recalled to writers' workshops where they produced pupils' books and teachers' guides for core subjects in grades 1 and 2.

In the Agricultural Vocational Education Project in Kyrgyzstan, a competence profile was prepared (see pages 81–3). Based on this profile, the curriculum was developed. Here is a section of the curriculum based on the extract of the competence profile we saw earlier.

Subject: sheep/goat breeding
1st semester: 1 hour/week, total 23 lessons

Topics	Skills and knowledge gained after a semester. The student:	Number of required lessons	Remark
1. Products of sheep and goat	Enumerates the products of sheep and goats and the criteria to assess quality and quantity.		
2. Types of sheep and goat	Differentiates between different types of sheep (wool, meat, milk, landraces, fat tail, fat rump) and goats (milk, meat, hair).		
3. Local breeds and condition	Explains the characteristics of local breeds and the present farming system.		

	Shows in which aspects local breeds are superior to exotic blood and where they need improvement.
4. Management	Gives an overview of the yearly cycle of sheep rearing and breeding. Characterizes the season and the work that has to be done.
5. Feeding	Assesses the nutrition needs for sheep in different ages, reproduction stage and performance. Enumerates 'musts' and 'don'ts' in sheep and goat feeding.
6. Breeding objectives	Makes breeding objectives for a local sheep and goat herd.

The curriculum framework is now becoming more detailed, but it still needs more development. We must now consider the content of the course, the methods of teaching and learning, and the learning materials which will be used.

DECIDING ON THE CONTENT, METHODS AND MATERIALS FOR A TRAINING COURSE

As we have seen, every course will have an overall framework, which is based on the knowledge, skills and attitudes/beliefs which learners need. Within this framework, there are learning outcomes which indicate what every learner should achieve by the end of the training course.

There is a direct relationship between the learning outcomes and the content of a course, as well as between each of those and the methods and the materials which are used to facilitate teaching and learning. This is shown in Figure II.3.1.

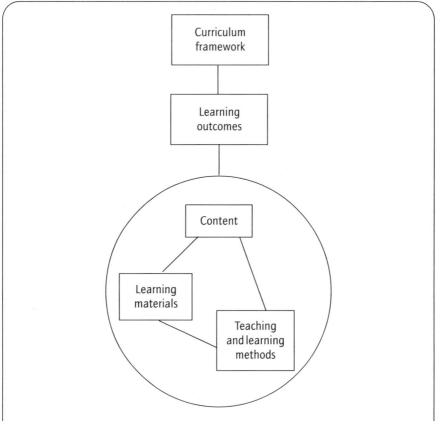

Figure II.3.1: A course consists of learning outcomes and content as well as the methods and materials which are used to facilitate teaching and learning

But learning outcomes only provide a guideline about *what* should be learned. The actual content of the course will describe *how* the learning will take place.

The content of training courses

There are two factors you should consider when identifying the content of the training course: selection and sequencing of the content.

Selecting the content

It is impossible to include everything in one training course. Even in long courses of several years, there is usually a lot of debate about what should be included. For a one-week course, selecting the content can be quite a headache. Very often, different stakeholders have strong views about the content of the course. For example, someone who has a background in animal husbandry will think about all their own knowledge and skills which could be useful to others. They would like to see all this in the course. This is true for experts in nutrition, literacy, forestry and so on. How can you find a solution?

If you have read this book carefully, you probably have realized already that following the PCD cycle will help you resolve this difficult question.

Instead of *starting* with the content of a training course, we started by thinking about *learning* and the *learning needs* in relation to the environment from which the learners come. Based on an analysis of the situation and the learning needs, you then identified, with other stakeholders, the knowledge, skills and attitudes/beliefs which the learners need to acquire. Based on this, you identified the aims and the learning outcomes of the course. If your learning outcomes are very clear, you should now find it relatively straightforward to choose the content of the training course.

Start with this useful technique: make a list of the content needed in order to help the learners acquire the identified knowledge, skills and attitudes/beliefs required by the learning outcomes. If there is too much content, divide it into three categories:

- ▶ must know
- ▶ should know
- ▶ could know (or 'nice to know').

All the knowledge that the learners *must know* must be included in the course content. Some of the knowledge that they should know, and a limited amount of what they could know can also be included. It is impossible to include everything!

Once you have selected all the knowledge, skills and attitudes, organize them into a sequence.

Sequencing the content

There are four basic rules for sequencing the content:

- ▶ Move from the simple to the complex. Remember the different levels of learning (page 97). For example, a training course on soil fertility could start off with a discussion on why crops sometimes fail to grow well, rather than starting out with complex explanations of the chemistry of commercial nitrogen fertilizers or of application rates of inorganic fertilizers.

▶ Use an existing logical organization. This may be chronological, topical or dependent on learning styles. For example, a training course on malaria prevention could be based on typical climatic features of the calendar year, and the way that this can lead to increases in numbers of mosquitoes, lower resistance in people living in rural areas, and subsequent rises in the likelihood of infection.

▶ Move from the known to the unknown. For example, a training course on environmental conservation could begin by asking participants to identify problems they have noticed in their own area which could lead to damage of the environment (such as careless rubbish disposal, lack of control of domestic animals, poor hygiene practices, etc). Abstract topics such as global warming could be addressed later as the understanding of participants grows on more familiar topics.

▶ Cover the content in the order of job performance. For example, a training course on food preparation and hygiene might follow the sequence in which a particular dish is prepared, starting with personal hygiene practices, washing, peeling and chopping food, methods of cooking, presentation of the food and learning points on storage of the cooked product.

Methods of teaching and learning

It has been said that teachers should think more about learner-learning than teacher-teaching. This is good advice to remember when you are deciding on the learning activities and methods of teaching and learning that you will use to deliver your training course. It means you should try to

▶ help the learners on your training courses learn about the subject
▶ help them enjoy the experience of learning so that they will feel like learning more when the training course has finished.

In other words, you should be an effective facilitator.

Let us say a few words about facilitation. A good facilitator is able to use a range of methods which can enhance the teaching or learning process. She or he also knows which combination of methods to use under which particular circumstances.

If you are an experienced trainer, then you may need to help others – who may be new to or less experienced in training – to learn how to use more participatory methods and approaches. You may want to organize a training course or workshop to train other trainers. We looked earlier at organization of workshops (pages 45–7), and many of the points there will help you. Here are a few more points you may find useful if you are facilitating a training event, whether it is a course for learners or a training workshop for new trainers.

A facilitator should

▶ understand the content of the course
▶ ensure that participants in the training are actively involved in the learning process
▶ be able to determine when understanding is not taking place and be prepared to act on behalf of the participants
▶ coordinate and help learners participate in learning activities which will help them to construct their own learning from the training course
▶ clarify meaning and help learners contextualize it
▶ enable learners to see how new knowledge can be applied in useful ways
▶ encourage learners to voice their opinions, raise questions and discuss issues with the trainer and with each other
▶ provide and distribute relevant information and learning materials to enhance learning
▶ together with the participants, monitor the group dynamics, communication processes and the achievement of learning outcomes
▶ be aware of conflicts or blockages to learning, and find ways of resolving these with the participants.

If you are a trained teacher or trainer, you have probably experienced and used different methods of teaching. On the other hand, you may have received no training at all. If this is the case, you can build your knowledge in several ways. If possible, try to attend in-service teacher training or training-of-trainers workshops where you can receive support. You can ask experienced teachers or trainers whom you know for advice. Try to read books about teaching methods (see the reading list on pages 163–4).

Here is a list of common teaching and learning methods which you may have seen, experienced or read about:

▶ practical activities (for example, going to the field, practising skills by doing tasks, using tools and equipment, etc.)
▶ questions and answers
▶ lectures or presentations
▶ visualization

- ▶ individual exercises and assignments
- ▶ opinion exchange and discussion
- ▶ problem-solving exercises
- ▶ demonstrations
- ▶ group activities
- ▶ case studies
- ▶ projects
- ▶ role-plays
- ▶ experiments
- ▶ simulations
- ▶ excursions.

On pages 119–33, you will find step-by-step instructions for some specific teaching methods which you can use in your training.

Teaching and learning materials

It is important to use a variety of teaching and learning materials because they can help to make the learning experience more effective.

Why do you need teaching and learning materials?

- ▶ Learners can relate well to visual things.
- ▶ Learners remember more of what they see than of what they hear.
- ▶ Learning materials create interest. They stimulate and appeal to the learner's natural motivation.
- ▶ Learning materials present information in ways which a verbal presentation cannot. They are versatile and offer great opportunities to widen the learning experience.

Examples of materials include posters, slides, photographs, TV and videos, handouts, overhead transparencies, drawings on a board, cartoons, written case studies, games and so on. Puppets or drama can be particularly effective at communicating complex or sensitive ideas. The more real your learning materials are, they more effective they will be. For example, many literacy-training programmes use real-life materials, such as official forms, newspapers, instructions and advertisements for medicines or other products, weights and measures and so on. These are reading materials which learners face in their daily lives, so using them on literacy training makes the course directly relevant to participants, which is very motivating.

Developing and producing learning materials

There is a difference between developing learning materials and producing them. Development of materials is the process of finding out what kind of materials will bring about learning most effectively, so that learners achieve the learning outcomes and the aims of the training course.

Production of materials, on the other hand, is the physical act of making materials. Some materials, like posters, can be produced very easily and cheaply. Others are expensive and require quite a high level of skill and resources, such as making a video.

Teaching and learning materials should be attractive, interesting, challenging, durable, economically viable to produce and well organized in terms of content to enhance the learning process.

Consider the following steps when you are developing teaching/training materials:

▶ Establish the purpose of the materials and the target audience.
▶ Decide the general types of material needed.
▶ Identify the learning outcomes which the materials will support.
▶ Decide the content which the materials will deliver, and which teaching methods will be used with the materials.
▶ Organize the presentation; choose an attractive format and style.
▶ Test prototype materials with learners and change the materials if necessary.
▶ Think of how you will assess whether the materials have been effective in your training course.
▶ Use the materials in your training course.
▶ Revise them if necessary.

Displaying and storing teaching and learning materials

You can buy ready-made teaching and learning materials or you can make them yourself. Either way, you need to display them.

Here are some simple ideas for displaying pictures and drawings:

▶ Stick them on the eight sides of an opened-up cardboard box
▶ Tape pieces of cardboard together to make a large display board
▶ Hang pictures or models from coat-hangers, or on sticks suspended from the ceiling. If you are teaching outside, you can hang these from a tree branch.
▶ Use string to hang pictures, like a clothes line. This is very useful outside, where you can use trees as your 'classroom walls'.

▶ Instead of paper, use other materials as backing to display your poster: for example, grass matting, cloth or thick cardboard.

▶ Make the backing more stable by fixing a thin piece of wood at the top and the bottom. Then you can roll up the whole display when you are not using it.

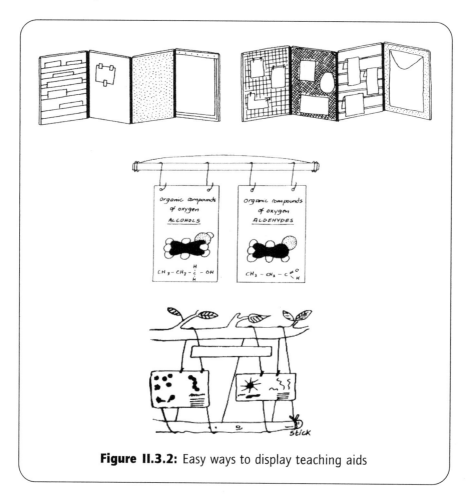

Figure II.3.2: Easy ways to display teaching aids

Vary any display of posters in your classroom, since your learners may lose interest in a display which has been on the wall for several months.

To keep your charts and materials safe, make a folding multi-board out of plywood or thick cardboard. You can use this to carry your materials and also use some of the boards to display your materials. If you close the boards carefully and tie them up with a belt or strap, you have an instant travelling display unit. This is very useful if you are moving from classroom to classroom or if you sometimes teach outdoors.

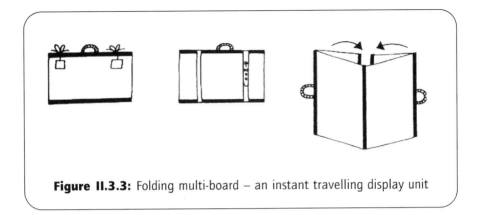

Figure II.3.3: Folding multi-board – an instant travelling display unit

In order to make your learning materials last, it is important to look after them well. Store them safely when they are not being used. Termites and mould are the main enemies of paper, so store posters and other paper materials in an airy cupboard over wooden racks. A metal cabinet will keep out most insects. If it is possible, it is a good idea to laminate posters. This means that they are coated in thin, transparent plastic and they will last for a very long time.

In this book, we cannot give detailed instructions for making different types of learning materials. There are many books which can help you to do this (you can find some suggestions in the reading list on pages 163–4). You could also ask other teachers or trainers to help you with ideas or with making learning materials which you can share.

MAKING A TRAINING PROPOSAL AND BUDGET

In some contexts, you may be required to prepare a concrete, written proposal for the training for those people or institutions who are responsible for allocating funding and resources. This puts into writing all the preparations you have done: written the learning outcomes, and selected suitable content, methods and materials for teaching and learning. A training proposal also ensures that you are prepared logistically and that you have enough resources to manage and run the training course.

Try to include all the following elements in your training proposal:

1. Name of the training course.
2. Proposed participants (number, names/positions) (and maybe also participants' role in the training process).
3. Proposed logistics (timing, location, etc.).

4. Rationale for the training (need, TNA findings, other situational factors).
5. Aim of the training.
6. Framework for the training which includes:
    *   specific learning outcomes
    *   content
    *   methods for teaching and learning
    *   learning materials
    *   other resources
    *   time frame.
7. Budget.
8. Evaluation procedure.
9. Plan for follow-up (relating this to other activities or future training events).

The person or group to whom you give your proposal will use certain guidelines and criteria to assess the quality of the proposal. Here are some examples of common criteria which may be used: you can use these to assess your own proposal before submitting it officially.

▶ What is the relationship of the proposed training course to the broad concepts or principles of the area in which you are working (health, natural-resources management, sustainable rural development)?

▶ What is the relationship of the proposed training course to the overall workplan for the organization or project in which you work? Is running this course feasible within existing resources (rationale, timing, participants and budget)?

▶ What is the relationship of the proposed training course to any existing human-resource development or staff-development plan (in terms of its contribution to institutional capacity-building, role and function of participants within their institutions)?

▶ How innovative or well-grounded is the training? (Can we consider it as a pilot or testing ground for new aims/learning outcomes, methods, materials or content? Is it based on a sound understanding of educational and technical theory and practice?)

▶ What will be the need for follow-up and support from internal or external persons?

▶ What is the potential for co-leadership or active participation from different stakeholders?

▶ Is the level (aim/learning outcomes/content) of the proposed training course appropriate for the actual capacity of the trainers?

▶ How cost effective will the course be?

Budgeting

Preparation of the budget for a training course depends on the source of funding. If you are working for an institution, there are probably standard procedures for making a budget. The following example provides you with some of the key elements you should remember.

Budgeting for a training course

Item	TNA	Design	Implementation	Evaluation/ report-writing	Total
1. Human resources (fees) • Teachers • Assistants • Secretary • Accountant • Others (cleaners, servers) • Prepare hall/classroom • Informants					
2. Accommodation, food (for the people above)					
3. Participants • Food • Accommodation • Refreshments					

4. Travelling
• Petrol, driver for:
  – Trainers
  – Participants					

5. Stationery, materials, facilities, rooms, etc.					

4 / Deliver and use new curricula

Now you have prepared the detailed curriculum, selected teaching methods, prepared learning materials, and your training proposal has been written, submitted and approved. There is one more important thing to prepare: the plan for your training sessions.

PLANNING LESSONS/SESSIONS

Good teaching and training requires good organization. We have seen already that the curriculum is the guide to the overall teaching and learning process. A lesson or session plan helps to ensure that the curriculum is delivered effectively and that the learning outcomes are achieved. Lesson planning is an important part of the curriculum development process.

All teachers and trainers should plan how to teach a lesson. Even trainers with many years of experience have to teach new topics or techniques or try new methods or materials. Apart from being a good way to organize your work, lesson planning encourages reflection. Before making the plan, think about how you approached training before, what went well, what did not work so well, and what aspects of your teaching you would like to change or improve. By reflecting on questions like these, you can plan and be prepared, and your teaching is likely to be more effective.

It is a very good idea to discuss your first draft of a lesson plan with a colleague – don't be afraid to receive and act on constructive criticism. You will learn a lot from the reaction of your learners as well when you actually try out the lesson.

A lesson or session plan is a detailed description which usually covers the following information:

▶ the class or group you teach (year, number of learners), what subject and topic, when the lesson will be held
▶ the main aim of the lesson (from your overall curriculum)

► the main learning outcomes (from your overall curriculum)
► a breakdown of the lesson into different elements. Allocate time to each element to make sure it fits into the lesson. The lesson may include:
  • an introduction of the topic, which includes finding out what your learners already know and a link to a previous lesson (if appropriate)
  • a presentation of the main theme, perhaps a demonstration or a practical activity for your learners
  • a conclusion, and a link to the next lesson
► a list of the teaching and learning methods you will use in each part of the lesson
► a list of the teaching and learning materials you will need for each activity
► a guide to how you will evaluate the learning in the lesson.

After the lesson, make notes which describe how the lesson went – what worked well, what could be improved and what you could do better or differently next time.

An example of a simple format for a lesson/session plan

Title: Location:

Duration: Aim:

Learning outcomes: By the end of the lesson, the learners will be able to:

•
•
•

Learning points	Resources	Method	Time (mins)
Introduction: Link to previous lesson			
Development: Main content of the lesson			
Conclusion • Review of main points, referring to learning outcomes • Evaluation			

Notes: (here you can add any additional information which is important, e.g. follow-up to the next lesson, special safety precautions, etc.)

A completed example of a lesson plan for an agriculture lesson:

Title: Observing a soil profile

Location: beside road outside school

Duration of lesson: 45 minutes

Aim: to demonstrate the different layers of soil found in a soil profile

Learning outcomes: by the end of the lesson, the students will be able to:

- identify the main layers of soil in the pit or profile
- explain why the soil appears to be made up of different layers
- describe the difference between these layers in terms of what they contain
- describe the likely characteristics of water and fertility of this soil
- explain why the layers have different colours
- apply this knowledge of soils when growing plants themselves in the garden

Key points	Resources	Method	Time
Introduction • Link to previous lesson on soil types. • Soils show differences in a vertical direction as well, forming a series of layers. Different layers of soil have different value for plant growth. • Topsoil is the best for plant growth as it contains most organic matter. You can recognize it by its dark colour, and the pieces of leaves, twigs and other vegetable matter. • Soils which have suffered from erosion or other damage may lack some layers, especially topsoil; this will affect the growth of plants as there may be fewer nutrients available for their growth.	Poster display of soil types from previous lesson. Samples of different layers of soil (dark topsoil, light subsoil, rocky parent material).	Presentation with visual aids of posters and soil samples. Explanation of demonstration. Warning about need for safety beside road.	15 minutes

Key points	Resources	Method	Time
Development • Demonstration of a soil profile and its different layers. • Appearance and value of the different soil layers for plant growth, and the relationship with water-holding capacity and fertility. • Soil layers can be seen because of the way in which rocks break down into soil; topsoil appears dark because it has been mixed over time with the remains of living things, and it is occupied by still-living things; subsoil has had less contact with living things, and the stones from the parent material have been broken down less; as you go down through the soil, the stones get bigger, and the influence of living things becomes less and less.	A ready-made soil profile – a bank beside the road outside the school.	Take class outside to roadside. Demonstration of the different layers in the soil profile. Group discussion.	20 minutes
Conclusion • Review of main points, referring to objectives. • Link to gardening practical on following day.	Classroom.	Return to class. Question and answer session.	10 minutes

Good planning is vital, but the delivery of a new or revised curriculum is the real test of whether learning can be achieved effectively. The delivery of the course is the moment when you, the learners and other stakeholders find out if the needs have been identified correctly, if the situation has been well understood, and if the design has been appropriate to meet these needs.

Even if a course is designed with the involvement of different stakeholders and great care is taken during each phase described in this book, you should always expect the unexpected when it comes to the training itself. This is because training, and learning, involves people, and the simple act of bringing a group of individuals together can have some unpredictable outcomes. Often, trainers assume that everyone comes to a training course with the same agenda. In fact, this is rarely the case, as the case study below shows.

Dealing with different expectations of training: an example from a VSO workshop in Malawi

As part of a curriculum development process, participants were invited to attend a pilot training course and make recommendations for finalizing a manual for future training events.

'After we had identified and invited the participants for the pilot training course, which was also a kind of editing workshop, we realized that the participants had different interests in the manual and we had to find a consensus to be able to continue with the training. We were shocked that the people were of such different opinion, since their main interest was exactly the same – to test a training tool for extension workers and others. We spent lots of time with discussions and provided one whole morning for groups' input for the different chapters that were taught the days before. We decided as a group how to proceed with the manual.'

VSO curriculum developer

A good lesson to learn from this is to build some additional time and flexibility into every training course. That way, you are prepared to respond to needs and perspectives which emerge during the course. Negotiation will be necessary in order to reach agreement on a common agenda, so good facilitation skills will be important. Openness, transparency and a willingness to listen are also vital when situations such as this occur. It is rare to find participants who really try to sabotage a training event completely if the training is approached in a participatory way.

MEETING CHANGING NEEDS DURING THE COURSE

During your planning, you identified the key learning outcomes and the types of experiences or activities which are likely to bring these about. As long as these learning outcomes are still relevant, then the trainer has an equal responsibility with the participants to see that these outcomes are achieved.

Sometimes, the learning outcomes or the teaching and learning methods may need to be reconsidered during the training. For example, the learning outcomes may be too challenging or too basic, or they may not match the expectations of the participants. Occasionally, unforeseen events take place, such as storms, lack of transport, buildings or equipment which fail to function. In all these cases, there is a need to make changes on the spot, but these changes should always be discussed with the participants. At some point, decisions need to be made. This may be the responsibility of the trainer alone or others may also be involved in the decision-making process. If you have accepted the basic principles of PCD, then you will realize that some of the burden is actually removed from the trainer, because the responsibility for the success of the course is shared more widely.

Sometimes it is very difficult to make major changes in the course design at a late stage. If the course design has been as participatory as possible, this should reduce the need for major changes. Remember, too, that there is no such thing as the perfect course. There are certainly good courses, however, and this book has been written to help you design them.

Here are a few more suggestions which you may find useful as you prepare to deliver your new or revised course for the first time:

1. Ensure that the trainers or teachers involved in delivering the course have all the necessary knowledge, skills and attitudes/beliefs them-selves. Many courses fail to be effective because teachers and trainers are not prepared well, or lack certain key skills. In some cases, it may be necessary to provide training for the trainers before the course, to help increase their readiness before the course is tested.
2. Ensure that all necessary resources and materials are available for the course delivery. This should have been dealt with in the planning stages, but it is worth mentioning again. There are many unfortunate examples of vital equipment being lost or missing at the final moment (one common mistake is to forget the fuel for the car, even though the car and driver have been organized!)
3. Have contingency plans. If you are going to carry out training where there is an unreliable electricity supply, don't rely on overheads or a

computer-generated presentation. Always have a backup, and if necessary be ready to cover course material in a different way from how you have planned.

4. Think about evaluation before testing the course. Be ready with questions such as:
    - Was the preparation for the course well done?
    - Has the course been effective, both during, at the end of, and beyond the end of the course?
    - Have the learning outcomes been achieved by all participants?
    - To what extent are the participants satisfied with different elements of the course?

    Evaluation is discussed in the next part of this book, and you will find many ways of finding out the answers to these questions in a participatory way.

5. Establish a recording system for each training that you carry out. You may need to report back to other stakeholders (such as managers) what happened during the course. The report should be meaningful, and ideally, follow the 'KISS' principle: 'Keep It Short and Simple'. Normally it should reflect the original training proposal (see pages 109–10), and probably contain the following components:

    i.   Title of the training.
    ii.   Details of actual participants (number, names/positions, and maybe also participants' role in the training process).
    iii. Actual logistics (timing, location, etc.).
    iv.   Activities carried out (summary of the training event, especially noting any differences between planned and actual).
    v.   Main results/outcomes of the training (for example, KSAB attained, processes developed, products created, action plans, issues and/or opportunities, etc.).
    vi.   Follow-up activities.
    vii. Plan for follow-up (relating this to other activities or future training events).
    viii. Need for follow-up support (financial, material or human inputs).

You might also add some further information as appendices. For example:

▶ actual budget
▶ original proposal for the training (Rationale for the training, aims and framework for the training and evaluation procedure can be dealt with by attaching the original proposal as an appendix.)
▶ teaching and learning materials provided for the course

You may also want to make your own record of what has worked well and what should be changed for the future, to help you improve subsequent trainings. Keeping a record is also a good way for you to reflect on the effectiveness of the training, which is part of your own learning process.

DELIVERING THE NEW CURRICULA: TEACHING METHODS

Now let's look at some specific teaching and learning methods which you may find useful as you deliver your new or revised curriculum. They have been tried and tested and adapted in many contexts, and they are a good way for you to get started.

If at first you feel that a new method or approach has not worked very well, do not give up. You will learn a lot the first time you try a new method, and this will help you improve or adapt it.

Participants in your courses may need to become familiar with different methods as well. Adults with little formal education may be unaccustomed to different ways of learning. Many learners, adults, young people or children, may only have experienced 'chalk and talk' teaching methods, so you must expect some surprise and even a lack of cooperation from them. Our experience is that most learners come to appreciate that a carefully-chosen range of teaching methods and materials can help them learn more effectively. However, this can take a little time, both for you and for them!

When you try out a new method, reflect afterwards on what actually happened. What worked well? What worked less well? If possible, ask someone (a professional friend or colleague) to observe a training session and give you feedback afterwards. If you have the facilities, you could even ask someone to make a video recording of one of your training sessions so that you can see yourself afterward. Most of us do not like to see ourselves on film in this way, but of course, this is what your learners see, so it is a good way to assess yourself as a trainer to help you improve.

Reflect on how you can improve your teaching practice. Try new methods. This is all part of the learning process. If you think of yourself as a learner, just as the participants in your training course, then you are much more likely not only to work in a participatory way but also to keep improving as a trainer.

The blackboard (or whiteboard)

We start with some tips on using the blackboard (or whiteboard), because this is the piece of teaching equipment which is most commonly used by teachers and trainers for writing and for drawing.

Always present your work neatly on the blackboard. Organize your work by dividing the blackboard into areas. Some rules to follow are:

▶ Move across the board gradually. Do not jump from one point to another.
▶ Underline headings and important terms and statements.
▶ Draw large, clearly-labelled diagrams which stand out from any notes.
▶ Use a stick or string to draw straight lines or circles.
▶ Use your chalk in different ways to create different effects (fat or thin lines, shading, etc.).
▶ If there are certain shapes which you need to draw regularly, make a template of thin wood or thick cardboard which you can draw around to make a neat diagram.
▶ When cleaning the blackboard, pull the duster across the board either horizontally or up and down; sweeping the board in all directions creates a dirty board and a lot of dust.
▶ Always clean the blackboard before another teacher comes to use it. If there is something you need to leave for your learners to copy, draw a line around it and mark it 'please leave'. In the same way, respect the wishes of other teachers.

Presentations

Why use presentations?
Part of every lesson involves presenting information to learners, but if you talk to your learners for a long time without involving them actively, you are likely to lose their attention. You need to motivate and interest them. Here are some ideas to help you.

What you can do
▶ Start the presentation by finding out what your learners already know about the topic. Ask questions which do not require only a 'yes' or 'no' answer to find out what they know.
▶ Ask your learners why they think they should learn about this topic. This can help them have some input into the aim and learning outcomes of the lesson.
▶ Try to relate the topic to what your learners are familiar with, either from a previous lesson or session or from their own experience. Use examples which they will find interesting.
▶ Do not include too much information.
▶ Remember that every group of learners is made up of individuals, each of whom has his or her own personal interests and way of learning.

Try to meet the learning needs and styles of each of your learners by using a variety of teaching methods.

▶ Use a range of different learning materials: the blackboard (or white-board) is very useful, but try to use posters, pictures and *real materials* (such as plants, foods, implements, tools, written materials such as official forms, etc.) if possible to create interest.

▶ Encourage your learners to become involved with the lesson material. Use demonstrations. Let your learners touch, smell, observe and draw the items under discussion: remember that learners forget most of what they hear and a lot of what they see. Doing leads to understanding.

▶ Give your learners a chance to take notes, either during the presentation, or immediately afterward. You could do this by dictating or by neatly writing notes on the board (see page 120). Older or educated literate learners can be encouraged to write their own original notes of the main points. Find out about the ability of your learners as soon as possible.

▶ Ask your learners to take some responsibility for their own learning. Encourage them to undertake projects, keep diaries, look for information from newspapers and books, listen to interesting information on the radio or the television, and observe the practices of daily life of their families and neighbours.

▶ Try to observe the reactions of your learners – this becomes easier as you get to know them. Ask questions regularly, sometimes to all learners, and sometimes to particular individuals. It is very helpful to know and address your learners by name, as this will help you to build up a good relationship with them, and it will increase their attention!

Brainstorming

Why use brainstorming?
▶ to generate a range of ideas from a group of people, quickly and effectively
▶ to overcome blockages in discussions
▶ as a warm-up exercise.

What you can do
1. Set the question you want the group to answer.
2. Present the question clearly to the group (ideally written up so everyone can see it).
3. Explain that:
   • everyone can contribute an idea
   • all ideas are valid – there are no wrong ideas

- all ideas will be recorded in a written form, either on cards which are posted on a chart, or directly onto a chart or board.

4. Ask the group to give ideas. If many people try to speak at once, try to moderate the discussion. Ask participants to raise their hands before speaking or to take turns in giving responses.

5. Keep going until a wide range of different ideas has been generated or until no new ideas are being offered.

6. The group may generate a lot of different ideas. It will probably be necessary to organize these ideas into categories (see 'Dealing with the output of group exercises', pages 127–8).

7. Thank the participants for their contributions.

8. Link the activity to the next topic or point in the lesson/session.

What do you need?
- flipchart stand and paper, or
- pinboard and cards, or
- chalkboard or whiteboard.
- pens/chalk, something to stick cards with.

Group formation and group activities

You will often need to organize your learners into groups in order to:

- discuss questions or assignments
- carry out experiments
- prepare learning or demonstration materials (posters, charts, models, games, displays, etc.)
- do practical work
- carry out a project
- prepare and perform a role play.

Pay careful attention to the way a group works together. One or two group members may dominate the activity, leaving other group members out of planning and decision-making in particular. Certain learners may always be given the least pleasant task to do, and other learners may use the cover of the group to avoid doing anything at all! Try to ensure that all group members share responsibilities and actions. Watch out for the situation where the most able learners always work together and those who have the most difficulty with their work always appear in their own group. This can be a good thing if the able group can do additional tasks while the trainer ensures that the less able group is given enough attention so that they complete the activity to a satisfactory level.

However, be prepared to re-organize some groups if they do not appear to be functioning well.

You can form learners into groups in many different ways:

1. According to existing seating arrangements – learners can work in pairs or in groups of three or four, just where they are sitting.
2. By random group formation – mix learners into new groups. One way of doing this is to count the individuals (1, 2, 3, 4, etc.) depending on how many groups you need. Or give out pieces of card with names or numbers of groups written on them, and your learners must find the other members of their group.
3. According to individuals' ability/experience – you may decide to form groups of learners who have the same level of ability or similar experience in a specific area of study.
4. According to individuals' interest in a given topic – if groups will be discussing different topics, learners can choose which group they would like to join.
5. According to individuals' interest in their own choice of topic – this is sometimes called 'open space', and learners can suggest their own topic for discussion. Groups are then formed according to the interest of each individual in the suggested topics, or individuals can still suggest other activities.
6. According to some other common feature such as age or sex.

Snowballing

This group exercise gets its name because it involves a small group gradually getting bigger during the activity – just like a snowball. (If you live in a country with no snow, there may be other examples more relevant to you, such as a dung beetle rolling up a ball of animal manure.) Snowballing generates intensive discussions on a specific question or statement, and is quite energizing.

Time: 30–40 minutes

What to do:
► Identify a very clear question or statement which the groups will discuss.
► Divide the learners into pairs. Tell them they have 5–10 minutes to discuss the question and produce a response on a paper or card. No plenary feedback is given at this point.
► Ask each pair to sit with another pair. The new groups of four should

discuss (5–10 minutes) their responses to the same question, and again produce a joint response on a paper or card.

▶ Each group of four now joins with another group of four, to make groups of eight. Again each new group discusses the same question (5–10 minutes). Each group now writes their responses on a flipchart or on cards and posts these on the wall. Groups of eight are usually big enough, or the discussion will take too long.

▶ Each group gives a short feedback on their response in the plenary session (10 minutes).

Merry-go-round

This group exercise generates ideas which are passed around in a circle. It is named after a very popular children's ride at fairgrounds, where model horses or small cars on a platform go round and round in a circle.

Time: 30 minutes

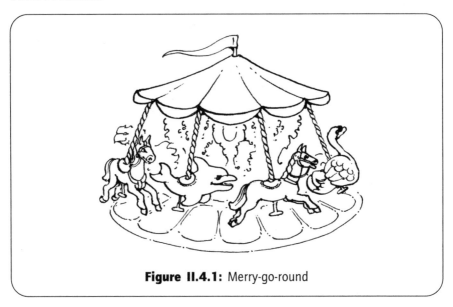

Figure II.4.1: Merry-go-round

What to do:
▶ Identify a clear question or statement which the groups will discuss.
▶ Divide the participants into groups of 6-8 participants each.
▶ Give each group member a paper and ask that each write down three things in response to the question. (Ask them to use short statements – the KISS principle [Keep It Short and Simple].)
▶ The papers are then circulated clockwise in the group.

► Each person reads the ideas on the paper and can then add a new idea.
► After a full round, the original paper comes back to its first writer.
► Each person now marks the idea he or she likes the most and then circulates the paper once more.
► After a second completed round, the ideas with the most marks are written down on cards and pasted on a flipchart paper, which is posted on the wall.
► The ideas are then discussed in plenary.

Variation:
► Instead of passing papers around, each participant may speak about his or her answer to the question for a limited time (for example, a maximum of one minute). He or she may not agree or disagree with previous responses, but should only add something new. If he or she has nothing new to add, then his or her turn can pass to the next person, again moving clockwise. One member of the group has the task of recording the main points and of giving feedback to the plenary. One group member should also act as chairperson to ensure that speakers keep to the time limit, and to see that discussions or debates do not start. The purpose of the merry-go-round is to generate new ideas, not to debate them.

Fishbowl
This group exercise allows a small group to discuss an issue while the other participants listen or join in if they like. It is carried out in a circle – just like sitting in a fishbowl!

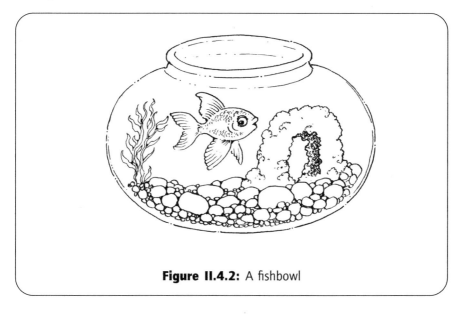

Figure II.4.2: A fishbowl

Time: depends on number of questions, but 1 hour maximum.

What to do:
▶ Prepare a set of questions or statements (five or six should be enough). Write them on a flipchart and cover them up with a paper.
▶ Arrange seven chairs in a small circle (the fishbowl). Place enough chairs for all other participants in a larger circle around the small circle – they are the 'frogs' (see Figure II.4.3).
▶ Six participants sit in the small circle. One chair is left free. The facilitator may also join the small circle if some encouragement is needed to get a discussion going. All other participants sit around in the outer circle.
▶ Uncover the first question. The participants in the inner circle should discuss this for 5–10 minutes. Those in the outer circle must remain silent.
▶ If someone in the outer circle (a 'frog') would like to make a comment, he or she can enter (or hop into) the inner circle and sit on the vacant chair to make the comment, but must then leave again. The others in the fishbowl must let him or her speak.

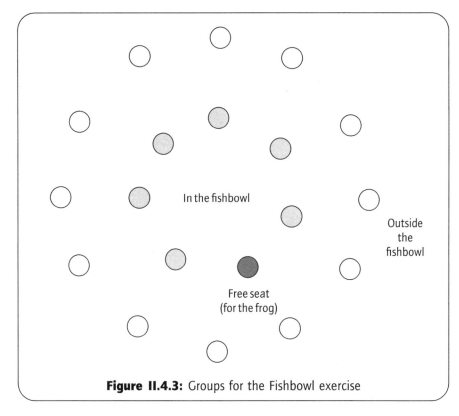

Figure II.4.3: Groups for the Fishbowl exercise

▶ After the given time, or if the discussion stops by itself, the group in the fishbowl leave their positions, and another group can take their place. Another question is revealed, and the same procedure is followed again. The same rules apply.

▶ Continue until all the questions have been addressed.

Short, focused discussions

Very often, your learners will need to discuss a very specific issue or question for a few minutes only. One difficulty with group discussions is that they often go on longer than you expected. So, give clear instructions on the output of the discussion and how long it should take.
Examples:

▶ Group of five persons, produce four answers, take 10 minutes
▶ Group of three persons, produce five answers, take 8 minutes
▶ Group of six persons, produce three answers, take 7 minutes.

You can form the groups in different ways (see group formation above). Always make the question(s) as clear as possible.

Dealing with the output of group exercises or brainstorming activities

You can do this in different ways. Here are some ideas.

▶ If the outputs have been written on cards and placed on a chart, they must be organized in some way. Cards usually work best with brainstorming activities (one idea per card, clearly written) because you can then move the ideas around after the exercise to form categories or groups of ideas. You can do this yourself, either in front of the group or during a break period. See which ideas are similar or identical and group them together on the chart. Draw a line around each group of ideas and give a name or title to this category which describes it clearly, for example, 'resources', 'methods', 'management', etc. Then have a short discussion on the categories of ideas in the plenary session.

▶ Or you can ask for volunteers from the participants to categorize the ideas, either on the spot or during a break. This is the better option, since the categories will be constructed according to the perception of the participants, but it may take longer.

▶ Another option is to ask each group to present its output on a chart. (Encourage the members of each group to make their charts clear and easy to understand.) A member of each group can then give to the plenary session a short feedback on what is on the chart. Set a time limit and ask the reporter not just to read what is on the chart but also to mention something about the process that is or her group went through to arrive at this output, and to highlight the most important points.

▶ A market of ideas is often more interesting than verbal feedback from group representatives. Each group should post its chart on the wall, and all participants can then spend around 20 minutes looking at all the posters. If someone has a comment or further idea, he or she can write the idea on a card or Post-it note and stick it on the chart. A member of each group can be available to answer any questions of clarification by individuals. Then have a final plenary session where you visit each chart with all participants, and quickly check the comments made by individuals. A short discussion can then take place. An alternative to the market is to turn the presentations into a game. One example is to have groups 'visit' each other, a bit like the 'home and away' teams in a football game. Using a scenario such as this also adds some fun and was used successfully at a trainers' workshop in Nairobi in Kenya.

▶ A more expressive output would result from asking the groups to present their outputs as a short play or a drama presentation. This can be a very effective method of feedback for topics which are sensitive. But it will also depend on the capacity of the group and their familiarity with such methods.

▶ Very often, some important points and issues are raised in these feedback sessions. But they are often not used effectively or may even be forgotten as the training moves on. Note any key outputs where all participants can see them and refer back to them when necessary. This can be done during the daily review, when it provides a good overview of what happened during a workshop.

Providing a demonstration

Why use demonstrations?

You can increase the likelihood of your learners remembering and understanding information by providing demonstrations. They can be done in the classroom or outside. In a demonstration, you or another person performs a technique under real or simulated conditions. Because your learners may not only hear, but also see, and perhaps touch and smell during the demonstration, they will feel more motivated and are likely to learn more effectively. Demonstrations appeal particularly to those with an activist learning style.

Demonstrations are particularly important if you are providing training in an area which involves practical activity. Your learners should have the chance to develop a range of practical skills as well as theoretical knowledge. They can actually see a skill or technique being used during a demonstration, and have the chance to ask questions or to give comments immediately. You may provide the demonstration yourself, or you may invite a local person with some expertise, such as a farmer, a community worker or an adviser.

Demonstrations can be useful in a number of ways:

▶ to teach a complex task or skill in a series of clear, practical steps
▶ to give your learners more confidence in a difficult technique before they try it themselves
▶ to show potentially dangerous practical activities in a safe environment.

Some points to remember about demonstrations:

▶ Always be sure you know (or the person demonstrating it knows) how to carry out a demonstration before you show your learners. Practise until you are sure how to do it.
▶ Demonstrations may require a lot of organization and preparation beforehand. Have everything prepared before you start a lesson, otherwise your learners will lose interest. Some demonstrations use expensive materials, so avoid waste (but try to avoid using expensive materials, as your learners may not have access to these in their situation).
▶ Involve your learners as much as possible during a demonstration. Ask questions regularly and check that they understand the procedure. You can also involve learners as helpers in demonstrations (as long as it is safe to do this) to increase interest for the whole group.
▶ Your learners should have a chance to practise the skill or technique after they have seen the demonstration. This will help them learn more effectively.
▶ In spite of the best preparations, sometimes demonstrations do not work. This reflects the reality of life and you can always point this out if something goes wrong. However, a good demonstration is a very effective learning experience, so try to ensure success if at all possible. You can also demonstrate how to do something in the *wrong* way, so that your learners can learn how not to do something as well as how to do it correctly. This is a good way to encourage learning and increases the opportunity for feedback and questions.

Practical activities

A lot of training for development is practical. Unfortunately, some education systems or training programmes give a lower value to practical work than to theory sessions. This discourages the use of practicals. It is important, however, that you give your learners as much opportunity as possible to practise skills and techniques. How can learners learn how to vaccinate a cow if they only learn about it in theory? They need to actually do it. If you are working within an institution where the timetable is set centrally, you may have to advocate to managers the value of practical sessions.

Practical activities can include the following:

▶ working on a school farm or garden, growing crops or rearing animals
▶ making and using simple machines and equipment
▶ doing experiments in the classroom, laboratory or field
▶ doing management tasks such as keeping records, accounts, etc.
▶ joining literacy groups
▶ taking part in or facilitating community-based activities, such as training, meetings, PRAs, etc.
▶ visiting practitioners (such as community extension workers or foresters) or beneficiaries (for example, farmers or non-literate adults)
▶ visiting experiments on-station or on-farm.

Practical activities should be well-planned and well-organized. You will need to brief your learners well beforehand and give support and advice as they carry out the activity. If you have a large number of learners on your course, you will almost certainly need to divide them up into smaller groups. It is very important to link the theory sessions with the practical experiences of the learners.

Just as with theory lessons, you need to have clear aims and learning outcomes for practical classes. Your learners should have a very clear idea about why they are doing the activity and what they are supposed to achieve. It is also important that they record what they have done in a practical notebook or diary. Observe your learners closely, offer advice where necessary, and encourage them to ask questions. If they are having difficulties, give them more chance to practise.

One difficulty with doing practical activities is that they are time-consuming. You need time to move to the practical area, field-site or village, to allocate tools and equipment, to do the activity and to bring all the equipment back again. For this reason, it is important to be organized and to allocate a realistic time for practical activities. Always leave enough time for cleaning up after practical activities. Encourage your learners to have a responsible attitude to materials, equipment and time, so that you are not running around at the end of every session, clearing up after your learners.

Project work

Why use projects?
Projects are a very useful way of allowing your learners to examine a topic or several topics in greater depth. They can encourage learners to increase their capacity to ask questions, make decisions and solve problems. Projects increase interest and motivation if you allow your learners to plan, carry out and write up their projects themselves, with help and guidance from you. Projects are more often used during longer training courses, where time is available for learners to develop their projects.

Types of project
One type of project could involve your learners going into the local community and finding out how local people carry out a certain activity, or what local people feel about a particular issue. This could involve a survey with interviews, or may require other information-gathering methods such as mapping, transects or ranking exercises used in PRA. Some possible topics for this type of project are:

▶ identifying the main farming systems in the area
▶ finding out about the different roles of men, women and children in agriculture or other forms of work
▶ discovering the views of local people about certain health or hygiene practices
▶ investigating the ways in which people market their produce
▶ making a business plan and carrying it out in order to produce and sell a product
▶ exploring the need for literacy and the benefits it could bring for specific groups of local people.

There are many other possibilities. Encourage your learners to generate their own ideas. They might get ideas from articles in the newspaper or items on the radio, or even from discussions at home.

Another type of project could involve your learners identifying a problem and designing a simple experiment to shed light on the issue. Examples of this from agriculture are:

▶ planting different varieties of crop
▶ sowing seeds in different ways (different spacings, different depths of planting)
▶ adding different amounts or types of fertilizer to crops
▶ supplying water in different volumes and at different times to crops
▶ sowing seeds directly in the field and sowing seeds in a nursery and transplanting.

In each of these cases, your learners can measure the plants as they grow and compare a number of variables, such as the time of emergence, growth rate, health, yield, etc.

Other examples of development-related projects could include:

▶ different approaches for raising tree seedlings in a nursery
▶ types of information which are most effective for community health or nutrition programmes
▶ analysis of different perspectives on land management by farmers and foresters.

When your learners undertake projects, it is important that you guide them during the early stages, as they may be new to the idea of project work. Each learner should be clear about the problem to be addressed, what he or she is trying to find out, and how he or she intends to carry out the project.

Ensure that the aim of each project is realistic. Project work is time-consuming, so they should not be too ambitious. It is better if you guide your learners toward projects which have a strong likelihood of a definite outcome. Encourage your learners to write up their project work as they go along. Read and comment on it regularly to help them keep on track. Your learners may need extra help with writing up their results, discussing them and drawing conclusions. The project report should be clear, simple and sensible.

Field visits

You will not be able to provide every learning experience in your training course. Your learners will understand concepts much better if they have first-hand experience of them. So, try to take your learners to locations, ideally within walking distance, where they can see, touch and smell things for themselves. You may know a local farmer who has dairy cows, or another farmer who is planting trees, or a new type of crop. There could be a site where soil-erosion is a particular problem, or a pit which provides a demonstration of a soil profile. There may be examples of community-based nutrition, literacy or credit and savings programmes which are using innovative methods.

It is important that a field visit serves an educational purpose, and is not just a sightseeing trip, although interest and enjoyment are important aspects of the field visit. Preparation is essential. Organize the visit well in advance and inform anyone who should know about it. Visits take time, and you may need to arrange longer visits in non-teaching times (perhaps afternoons or weekends), but discuss this with your learners first – some of them may have other commitments.

To prepare for a visit, always discuss the topic with your learners in advance. You could then ask them questions which they should answer as a result of the visit or give them a written sheet which they should complete. During the visit, ask your learners questions and encourage them to ask questions as well. This is part of the process of reflecting on experience. When you return to the training venue, have a review of the visit as soon as possible. In order to achieve concrete learning outcomes, ask your learners to develop ideas or principles based on what they have experienced, and then to make a simple action plan to show how they will apply what they have learned in reality.

5 / Develop and refine PCD evaluation system

Evaluation is an essential and continuous process. Often, evaluation is treated as if it is the final stage of curriculum development. However, curriculum development, and particularly PCD, is a cycle, not a linear process with a beginning and an end.

Evaluation should be an integral part of every stage of the cycle. Earlier in this book, we looked at the first workshop in the PCD cycle. One of the points covered there is evaluation. We have stressed in this book that it is important to think about evaluation at every stage of PCD.

If you have followed the PCD process, you considered how to monitor your course and how to evaluate the training and learning while you were developing your curriculum. So once you have delivered your new or revised training course and as you continue the PCD cycle, you are refining your evaluation system.

But first, let us look at what evaluation means in the context of PCD.

WHAT IS EVALUATION IN PCD?

When you evaluate a course, you are looking at what the curriculum is worth to those who are involved in its development, how well the curriculum is working, and how it can be improved, for present learners and for future ones. Evaluation can ask whether the aims of the curriculum and the learning outcomes have been achieved and how. It can also ask what difference this has made to the learners and to their lives, their work and their relationships to others.

Evaluation should examine the values of the curriculum being used, including the nature of the content of the learning (what knowledge is worthwhile?) and of the aims themselves (what *should* this programme of education and training achieve?).

Evaluation is not assessment. Assessment measures the performance of individual learners and the knowledge, skills and attitudes/beliefs they have acquired.

Try to formulate the methods, criteria and indicators for evaluation very early in the PCD cycle. Information needs to be collected and analysed, and conclusions drawn. All these activities should be carried out in a participatory way.

WHY DO YOU NEED TO EVALUATE TRAINING?

Evaluation can help you to define the learning outcomes more sharply, remove unnecessary training content, ensure that training methods meet the training needs of trainees and reduce training costs.

Evaluation can be carried out at different times.

Summative evaluation looks at whether aims and learning outcomes have been achieved. It is usually done soon after the end of the training programme, since the information needs to be obtained while it is still recent in the minds of those involved.

Impact evaluation is carried out when enough time has passed for longer-term effects to emerge. In particular, time is needed to allow the views of those involved in a training event to become clear and be put into perspective.

Try to establish an ongoing process of assessing and reassessing the progress being made throughout the course, the direction in which the course is heading, and the speed at which the aims and learning outcomes are being achieved. This is also called **monitoring**. The aim of monitoring is to provide the basis for course improvement, to determine the need for modification and ultimately to lay the foundations for future planning. It is a continuing process of critical reflection on experience leading to action.

Although you will usually monitor continuously throughout the course, often in association with the learners, try to create time during a course for specific opportunities for reflection, review and assessment. Throughout the course, check progress and what still needs to be done. By highlighting the areas which are successful and identifying those which need revision, you can adapt and improve the course as you go along.

WHO SHOULD BE INVOLVED IN CURRICULUM EVALUATION?

Effective and participatory evaluation is a key to successful development of the curriculum. Participation in evaluation gives the stakeholders access to the decision-making process by enabling them to have a say in what is being done now and what will be done in the future. Participation also requires and encourages commitment. If the stakeholders are involved in the design of the curriculum, they should also participate in the design and implementation of the evaluation of that process. Their increased motivation will help to make certain that the outcomes of the evaluation process will be worthwhile and lead to concrete results.

Traditionally, objectivity has been seen as an essential element of evaluation. A challenge when evaluating training courses is that stakeholders can find it difficult to stand back and see what is actually going on. Most forms of evaluation are undertaken by outside agencies in order to achieve impartiality and objectivity.

However, education and training is designed to meet human needs and these are, by their very nature, subjective. Learning involves the whole person, including feelings – such as, for example, learner satisfaction or confidence. As a result of this changing view about learning, different forms of evaluation are now becoming more common. (Some examples which you may find useful are given later in this section.) For this reason, many training programmes are now evaluated both internally by the participants and stakeholders and externally by outsiders.

Internal evaluations are usually conducted by those most directly connected with the curriculum, such as teachers, learners, policy-makers and education experts (for example, staff from the ministries of education, health or agriculture, or from academic institutions). This ensures that the evaluation has credibility, since the informants have first-hand working knowledge of the programme.

In practice, you, as a trainer or teacher, are probably evaluating your work all the time, especially if you reflect on what you do. You will often do it almost unconsciously or informally, when observing or talking with learners. Doing this kind of evaluation in a conscious way will make it more effective.

Learners also can be active evaluators. It is sometimes difficult to involve the learners in the evaluation process, partly because of teacher–learner relationships and partly because learners often feel that they themselves are the subject of the evaluation, rather than the curriculum. Being involved in the evaluation puts the learners on an equal basis with the teachers and enables them to see learning for what it is. Such evaluation is an important part of the learning process. Through it, the learners may see how much progress they have made, what measures of achievement they can use for themselves, and how much further they have to go before they reach their own goals. Instead of being just a 'carrot or stick', this type of evaluation can be a strong motivating force in the learning process.

External evaluations are usually undertaken by external agencies, such as examination boards or independent evaluators. An external evaluator is likely to have a higher degree of independence and objectivity, and often wider experience of other courses and programmes. Such evaluators are usually brought in from outside the situation in which the curriculum is being developed.

This can be a worrying period for trainers, as there is a fear that the evaluation may be critical and lead to undesirable consequences. This is unfortunate, because external evaluations can be very helpful and constructive. You can learn a lot from what has worked well and from things which have not gone so well. It is helpful to have someone highlight these and help you and others to learn useful lessons.

It is important that external evaluators take into consideration a wide range of views about the purpose of the programme from everyone involved with its development, rather than making their own judgements. One problem with external evaluations is that they are very often based on the results of examinations and tests given to the learners. In these cases, the examiner has the power over the learners since the examiner decides what will be assessed and how. Assessment does not need to be a one-way process, however. Teachers and trainers may assess the learners; equally, the learners may assess their teachers and trainers. Again, learners can assess themselves and their peers. The idea of peer- and self-assessment is becoming more popular, although in many formal training and teaching institutions, these innovative kinds of assessment are not always fully recognized or accepted.

In a PCD approach, those who have developed the curriculum need to know how well it is working. Regular review meetings of the stakeholders are useful in monitoring, and their involvement in the summative and impact evaluations is also necessary.

WHAT SHOULD BE EVALUATED?

There are two main approaches to evaluation.

▶ Some evaluators consider only specific aspects of the system – for example, the methods of teaching and learning – or the achievement of specific learning outcomes, and the knowledge, skills and attitudes/beliefs which have been acquired by learners. This is sometimes known as 'objective-led' evaluation.

▶ Other evaluators prefer to take a broader view in order to provide a basis for present and future curriculum development. This means that the evaluation is about a full understanding of the educational process. This type of evaluation may need to be more descriptive, interpretative or judgmental. It is often described as 'illuminative', since its effect is rather like shining a bright light into all aspects of the training and learning process.

It is necessary to monitor and evaluate the entire curriculum-development process at regular intervals and to involve as many relevant stakeholders as possible. You will need to decide what kind of information should be collected, and how and by whom it should be collected, analysed and interpreted.

If you and others involved in designing the training course have expertise in methods of evaluation, then you can advise and, in some cases, train other stakeholders in the technical skills of evaluation. The capacity of different stakeholders to participate in the evaluation process will then be improved, as will their capacity to make decisions more effectively. You might work as co-ordinator or facilitator of the evaluation process, but try to find ways to share control and involvement in all phases of the evaluation with other stakeholders.

AN EVALUATION APPROACH

Evaluation often seems very complicated. Certainly it takes some practice and experience to become a good evaluator: and a very useful approach to educational evaluation which can guide you is the CIPP approach developed by Stufflebeam. CIPP stands for context, input, process and product. This provides a systematic way of looking at many different aspects of curriculum development. There is a risk, however, that it may be directed only by experts or outsiders, and for this reason it is vital for you to identify ways in which your stakeholders can be meaningfully involved.

The CIPP model provides a series of questions to help you to evaluate the complete learning process. Like all models, it is a limited tool if you stick

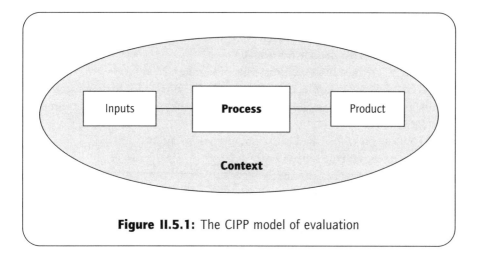

Figure II.5.1: The CIPP model of evaluation

very rigidly to the questions below. Try to pool your imagination and insight with others' in order to adapt it to your own context. Here are some sample questions.

Context
► What is the relation of the course to other courses?
► Is the time adequate?
► What are critical or important external factors (network, ministries)?
► Should courses be integrated or separate?
► What are the links between the course and research/extension activities?
► Is there a need for the course?
► Is the course relevant to job needs?

Inputs
► What is the entering ability of learners?
► What are the learning skills of learners?
► What is the motivation of learners?
► What are the living conditions of learners?
► What is the learners' existing knowledge?
► Are the aims suitable?
► Do the learning outcomes derive from aims?
► Are the learning outcomes SMART?
► Is the course content clearly defined?
► Does the content (KSAB) match learners' abilities?
► Is the content relevant to practical problems?
► What is the theory/practice balance?

▶ What resources/equipment are available?
▶ What books do the teachers have?
▶ What books do the learners have?
▶ How strong are the teaching skills of teachers?
▶ What time is available, compared with the workload, for preparation?
▶ What knowledge, skills and attitudes do the teachers have, related to the subject?
▶ How supportive is the classroom environment?
▶ How many learners are there?
▶ How many teachers are there?
▶ How is the course organized?
▶ What regulations relate to the training?

Process

▶ What is the workload of learners?
▶ How well/actively do learners participate?
▶ Are there any problems related to teaching?
▶ Are there any problems related to learning?
▶ Is there effective two-way communication?
▶ Is knowledge merely transferred to learners, or is it used and applied by them?
▶ Are there any problems which learners face in using/applying/analysing the knowledge and skills?
▶ Is the teaching and learning process continuously evaluated?
▶ Is teaching and learning affected by practical/institutional problems?
▶ What is the level of cooperation/interpersonal relations between teachers/learners?
▶ How is discipline maintained?

Product

▶ Is there one final exam at the end or several during the course?
▶ Is there any informal assessment?
▶ What is the quality of assessment and what levels of KSAB are assessed?
▶ What are the learners' KSAB levels after the course?
▶ Is the evaluation carried out for the whole PCD cycle?
▶ How do learners use what they have learned?
▶ How was the overall experience for the teachers and for the learners?
▶ What are the main lessons learned?
▶ Is there an official report?
▶ Has the teacher's reputation changed/improved as a result?

METHODS TO EVALUATE THE CURRICULUM

There are many ways to evaluate the curriculum. Here are some common ways. You could use several of these in combination with each other:

► discussion with participants
► informal conversation or observation
► interviewing learners individually (using the techniques described earlier on pages 75–7)
► evaluation forms
► asking colleagues to observe you teaching in class
► video-taping your teaching (micro-teaching)
► organizational documents
► participant contract
► performance test
► questionnaire
► self-assessment
► written test.

ASSESSING LEARNING

So far we have been discussing evaluation of the overall curriculum. As part of the overall evaluation process, you also need to find out if the learners are actually learning (changing their behaviour) as a result of the training. This will show you and others whether the training has been effective. Assessment is a means of finding out what learning is taking place. As well as specific knowledge and skills, you might also like to measure other changes in behaviour related to personality, social skills, interests, learning styles, etc.

There is a lot of debate about how to assess learning and especially about how to evaluate performance. The learning outcomes give you guidance on what to assess, because they are written in terms of what the learners should be able to do. Based on these learning outcomes, it is very useful to identify all the activities and skills which the learners will carry out, the conditions under which they will perform these activities, the possible results which might be obtained, and the standards by which their performance will be measured.

The measurement itself can be done in different ways. You can ask the learner to:

▶ recall or remember facts or principles (for example, ask the question 'what is . . . ?')

▶ apply a given or recalled fact or principle (for example, ask the question 'how does this fact or principle help you solve a particular problem?')

▶ select and apply facts and principles to solve a given problem (for example, ask the question 'what do you know that will help you solve this problem?')

▶ formulate and solve his or her own problems by selecting, generating and applying facts and principles (for example, ask the question 'what do you see as the problem here and how can I reach a satisfying solution?').

As you move down this list, the questions become more complex and concern learning at a higher level (see page 97). Try to encourage higher-level assessment questions, particularly by helping learners to identify problems themselves. This links to a good teaching practice we mentioned earlier – that of being indirect, rather than giving all the answers (or giving all the problems!).

Once again, we need to stress the importance of participation in assessment. As part of a PCD cycle, you should involve your learners both in the development of learning outcomes and, as much as possible, in their own assessment. In many education systems, assessment is used as a tool for comparing learners for selection purposes (progression to a higher level of education, higher rewards, etc.). It is much better if learners are clear about what they need to learn and also are clear about what they have learned by setting their own targets and monitoring their own progress. Of course, teachers and trainers should advise the learners, and guide them in order to help them learn: this is a key role of the teacher.

ASSESSMENT TOOLS

When you think about assessment tools, you will probably think about tests and exams, because these are so commonly used. Often, certificates or other qualifications are not awarded unless the learners pass tests. Among educationalists, there is now a growing realization that pass-and-fail testing is not actually very helpful. If a learner fails, then what is the point of the training course? Surely the whole purpose of training is to bring about learning, not to bring about failing! This is why a lot of training programmes now focus on competences (see pages 80–3).

Whatever approach to assessment you use, the most important thing is that learning does take place and that different stakeholders, particularly the learners, see and understand clearly what they have learned, and what they need to do to learn more.

1. Objective tests

Many teachers and trainers try to make sure that at least part of the assessment is objective and free from bias. Questions in an objective test have only one correct answer. This makes writing such tests quite difficult!

Bear in mind that objective tests tend only to assess lower levels in the domains of learning (see pages 96–7), particularly knowledge and comprehension. Also, it is difficult to set objective tests for training courses which are very experiential or practical.

Five types of objective test are commonly used:

1. short-answer questions
2. completion questions   involving supply
3. alternative-response questions
4. multiple-choice questions
5. matching questions   involving selection

The way in which these questions are set is crucially important. It is always a good idea to pre-test questions on colleagues or a sample of learners. All public-examination questions are pre-tested to ensure that the answers are those which are expected.

Here are some examples of each type of question from materials produced by VSO volunteers and their national colleagues.

Examples of objective tests
i) Short-answer questions
Q. What is the pH of a soil described as neutral?
Q. When written in full words, what does HIV stand for?

ii) Completion questions
Q. In a maize crop, purple coloration of leaves, reduced yields and poor root growth are likely to be caused by a shortage of _____.

iii) Alternative response questions (for example, true or false)
Q. Are the following statements TRUE or FALSE?

1. Malaria is caused by mosquitoes.
2. Not all species of mosquito can transmit malaria.
3. Natural immunity to malaria can be developed after one attack.
4. Malaria can be eradicated with drugs.
5. Patients with malaria only die after a prolonged illness.

iv) Multiple-choice questions
Circle the letter of the correct answer.

Q. The correct name for a young hen is a

A   chicken
B   pullet
C   cockerel
D   poultry.

Q. If you are HIV antibody negative, this means you

A   are immune to HIV
B   need not change your sexual behaviour
C   have not come into contact with HIV
D   are infected with HIV.

v) Matching questions
Q. On the left below are listed four nutritional components. Write the letter of that one found in particularly high proportions in the types of food listed below on the right.

Nutrient	Food	
A. Calcium	1. Potato	———
B. Vitamin C	2. Liver	———
C. Iron	3. Milk	———
D. Starch		

2. Restricted and extended-response questions

These questions differ from objective tests because the answer cannot be predicted exactly, although obviously certain information is expected in the answer. Restricted-response answers are restricted by content and also by the way they are set. They are normally concerned with a small aspect of the subject area and therefore target only certain learning outcomes. The way in which the question should be answered is also specified, for example: 'list five factors', or 'explain in no more than two paragraphs'.

> Q. Draw two isomers of the organic compound with the formula C_4H_{10}.

> Q. Briefly explain three main ways in which people can become infected with HIV.

Extended-response answers, also called essays, have fewer restrictions on content and format. There may be restrictions on length and time allowed, but the content can be as wide as the examiner decides. This of course makes marking them much more difficult. Although less objective tests take longer to mark, they do take much less time to set. This will be an important factor when you decide what proportion of each type of question you will use in an examination.

> Essay question: Protection is a major function of packaging. Discuss the different types of hazards from which products must be protected.

> Essay question: Many writers have portrayed women to be as important as men in society. Discuss this with reference to any three books you have read on this course.

3. Practical skills testing

In many training courses, at least half the learning time is allocated to practical work. This should therefore be reflected in the assessment procedure.

In order to assess a skill, you need to break down the skill into its component parts. This is known as skill analysis. The various parts can then be assessed in order to indicate whether the learning outcomes have been achieved. If you have developed learning competences, then you can also provide an opportunity for learners to demonstrate the level of their competence. You will need to check and ensure that the learning outcomes are well written so that the assessment is valid.

Areas of practical work that can be assessed are:

▶ skill in observation and recording observations
▶ ability to assess and interpret the results of practical work
▶ ability to plan practical procedures and techniques for solving particular problems

► manipulative skills
► attitudes towards practical work.

There are a number of assessment methods which can be used for practical skills:

► set exercises
► project work
► making a portfolio (a collection of products of the learner)
► course work
► oral questioning
► assessment by impression (observation).

Practical assessment is usually done internally, since it is time-consuming, and should be done on a regular basis. The teachers or trainers assess the learners and then either use the results themselves or, in the case of public examinations, forward the results to an examination board. The tests may be moderated by an external examiner to ensure that standards are comparable between different institutions.

ASSESSING ATTITUDES AND BELIEFS

In development activities, the attitudes and beliefs of everyone involved are absolutely critical. Your attitudes, beliefs and values as an educator are bound to affect the way in which you work and how you relate to others. They will certainly affect the way you view, understand and practise participation in your work and in your life. If certain attitudes are required in order to work effectively with people, how can these be learned, and even more problematic, how can they be evaluated? How can you assess areas of learning such as

► participatory diagnosis and solution of problems
► implementation of solutions
► the ability to make and take opportunities and to be creative
► willingness to work with poor and marginalized people
► the commitment and motivation of an individual?

Objective testing does not reveal much about the attitudes and beliefs of learners.

Instead, think about how you can use assessment to get to know the learner, and how you can encourage the learners to know themselves. Very often, the results of assessment are used as a means of selection for future education or employment. What can you know about a learner who has a grade A? Perhaps that learner has proved to be very good at answering questions – but what is that learner really like? What does she or he believe? How does she approach her work? Similarly, a learner who achieves a number of set criteria or competences has proved to be capable of these, but what else can she or he do?

Because of difficulties like this, there is a movement toward a more complete assessment than one final grade or a pass certificate. This is the learner profile, where those teachers and trainers who have come to know the learner can comment and provide indicators of performance over a long period in many different areas of the training. The learners themselves can also contribute to the profile by assessing themselves. This is becoming an increasingly common technique for staff development and appraisal.

EVALUATING TRAINING EVENTS

Just as there are useful tools for assessment of learners, there are also some very useful practical and participatory tools which can be used for evaluation of a training course, either during it or at the end. Here are some examples.

1. Evaluation dartboard

This is a very useful tool to gauge participants' feelings on a range of issues. On a large piece of paper, draw the shape of a dartboard, as shown below. Decide which aspects of the event you wish to evaluate. (You could also ask participants to suggest what aspects **they** would like to evaluate.) Participants should make a mark in each segment of the dartboard according to their level of satisfaction. The closer the mark is to the middle of the board, the higher the satisfaction. The further away from the middle, the lower their satisfaction. After participants have placed their marks, you can discuss the result. This method provides a snapshot of feelings at a particular time. It can be used either at the end of or during a training event or workshop. However, it is not very useful for evaluating past events or processes.

For example:

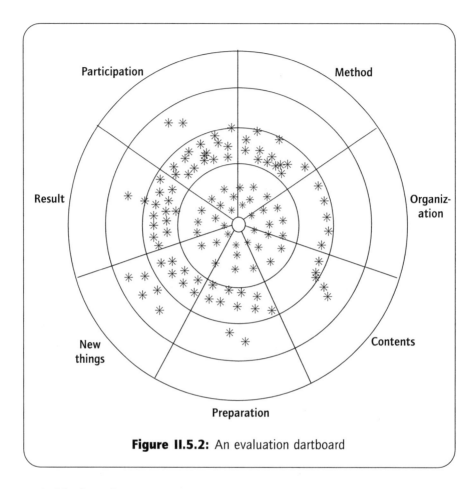

Figure II.5.2: An evaluation dartboard

2. Spider's web

If you are working with a small group, it is often very useful to monitor processes. This tool encourages discussion between group members about how an event is progressing over several days, or to consider the overall learning process. The spider's web is a series of lines running outward from a central point. Each line should relate to a separate criterion, such as level of participation or working environment, and be answered in response to a specific question. If participants are familiar with this type of evaluation, it is best if they select the criteria themselves through a discussion.

The group should then agree on a scale on each line, and discuss the extent to which that criterion (such as level of participation) is having an impact. When this has been done, a mark is placed on each line at the appropriate point. When this has been done for all criteria, another line can be drawn connecting all the points.

This exercise can then be repeated for the same criteria at different stages of the training or workshop. After several times, the diagram will look like a spider's web. The group can discuss what they feel about changes mapped on the web – some criteria may be having an increasing or decreasing impact – and what measures could be taken to improve or sustain the process.

For example: To what extent has our learning so far been affected by these different criteria?

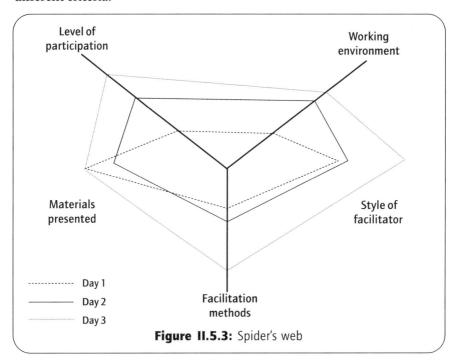

Figure II.5.3: Spider's web

3. Moodometer

This is a very simple and well-known evaluation tool. On a large piece of paper, make a diagram like this:

'My feeling about the course/workshop at the moment is:'

☹☹	☹	😐	☺	☺☺
	× × ×	× × × × × × × × × ×	× × × × × × × × × × × ×	× × × × × × × × ×

Figure II.5.4: Moodometer chart

Each participant places a cross under the picture which represents how he or she feels at that particular moment. This gives a very visual impression of how participants are feeling at a particular time either during or at the end of a workshop. The result should be discussed to elicit suggestions on improvements or changes.

4. Written comments

Evaluation tools which require participants to place only a mark on a paper can be very useful because they are quick and give an instant visual impression. However, they are limited in the amount of information they give. They do not allow participants to express their feelings in more detail. One simple way to encourage participants to express their views in an anonymous way (if that makes them feel more willing to be open) is to hand out different coloured cards. On one card, participants could write positive comments such as the following:

► what they liked most during the event
► the most important thing they learned
► what they will apply when they go back to their workplace.

On another colour of card, participants could write less positive comments:

► what they liked least about the event
► what they would like to be changed before the next similar event
► what they did not find at all useful about the event.

After writing on the cards, participants can stick their cards onto a wall or large paper. The facilitator or a small group of participants can then categorize the cards into key points, which could be discussed. Again, this tool can also be used during a workshop, for example at the end of a day, so that it could give the organizers a chance to respond, if that is possible. It helps if you explain to participants that it is not always possible for every comment to be addressed. The organizers will try to do the best they can with the resources they have available.

5. Process versus product

There is often criticism of training courses or workshops that a product was achieved, but at the expense of the process, for example by minimizing participation. On the other hand, it frequently happens that an event which is very strong on process (lots of participation) may fail to achieve a high-quality or expected product.

This evaluation tool enables participants to express their feeling about the combination and balance of process and product.

Draw a simple graph on a large piece of paper (see the black arrow and axes in the diagram below). Participants are then asked to place one cross on the graph according to their perception of both the process and the product.

For example:

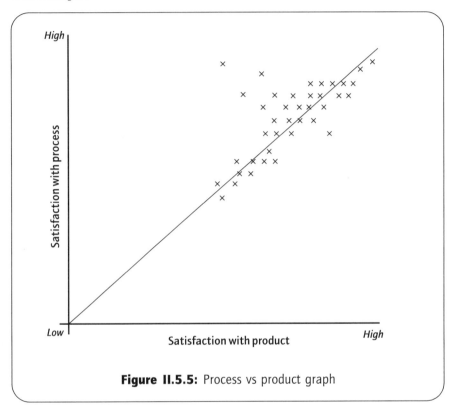

Figure II.5.5: Process vs product graph

QUESTIONNAIRE

Probably the most common tool used to evaluate training courses is the questionnaire. It is a good method, but it does depend of course on the quality of the questions. Writing good questions takes some practice. Poorly-prepared questionnaires may provide very misleading information. Often, the questionnaire is designed so that the participant reads a statement and then makes a mark to show if he or she agrees strongly, has no opinion or disagrees strongly with the statement.

Statements refer usually to items such as the course content, teaching and learning methods, materials, course organization, logistics and so on. In this way, the participant can quickly respond to various aspects of the course. If only marks are used, it can certainly be anonymous. Each questionnaire reflects the view of only one participant (unless you ask groups to answer the questionnaire) so it does mean that you will have to read all the returned questionnaires and make a small statistical analysis of the responses. This may be time-consuming, but it can also be a useful way to show how participants have validated the course.

You may also include a blank section in the questionnaire where the participant can make comments, to allow more freedom of expression and greater subjectivity. You might also ask participants to state their most valuable piece of learning from the course and also what they will put into action when they return to their workplace. Statements such as these can be very useful when planning future courses and also for monitoring impact of training courses if you follow up participants later through a tracer study. If you do ask participants questions such as these, then it may be more valuable if the exercise is not anonymous, so that you can follow up individuals at a later date.

6 / Maintain the PCD process

In this book, we have talked a lot about change. PCD is all about change, because it is about learning. Change can take place in individuals and also in institutions. Very often, we see individuals changing their personal behaviour quite dramatically, but unfortunately then coming up against institutional barriers and systems. Sometimes this is just bureaucracy. In other cases, it is because key persons in a system do not want to give up power or to allow others to be empowered. For this reason, it is important to think about PCD as an integral element of wider organizational change. Organizational development is critical for successful PCD. Unless organizational structures, systems, management and culture are open to a transformative approach to learning, it will be difficult to use a PCD approach.

A key strength of PCD however, is that it is flexible and dynamic, and is intended to work over a long period of time. It is not a one-off event. Although some parts of a system or an institution may not provide an enabling environment, there is always the possibility for change, as we saw in some of the examples presented in Part I, especially the example from Hungary on page 39.

Here is an example which gives an overview of a complete PCD cycle as it was planned by a VSO curriculum developer in The Gambia. This example is useful because it contains indicators, which allow the process to be monitored.

Revision of basic cycle curriculum: July 2001 to September 2002 (Julia Sander)

	Activity	Time – venue	Provisional date	Persons involved Critical assumptions	Indicators
1.	Review current Basic Cycle curriculum and instructional materials		Before end of July	Curriculum unit Teachers, parents employers	Survey conducted and report written Teachers, parents and employers give their views Recommendations made for new curriculum
2.	Preparation of draft curriculum format Grades 1–4 Knowledge, skills and attitudes identified		Before end of July	Curriculum staff (CREDU) *Staff available*	Draft curriculum format prepared by CREDU
3.	Discussion of proposed curriculum format with SMT at Department of State for Education (DoSE) personnel	To be arranged DoSE	Before end of July	SMT Curriculum Director Consultant and VSO volunteers	SMT have input into curriculum format Approach to curriculum is agreed
4.	Identify stakeholders		Before end of July	Curriculum staff	Stakeholders identified
5.	Sensitize stakeholders to new curriculum format Present survey of current curriculum	(Gambia College) (1-day workshop)	To follow meeting with SMT Before end of July	Curriculum staff Personnel from Department of State for Education and Gambia College	Stakeholders understand the principles of the new curriculum and have opportunity to input The findings of the curriculum survey are discussed

Activity	Time – venue	Provisional date	Persons involved	Indicators
			Critical assumptions	
			West African Examination Council SQAD (Inspectorate) INSET Lower Basic School principals Principal Education Officers (regions) *Venue and funding available*	
6. Prepare budgets for workshops and other activities Submit to Project Co-ordinating Unit for approval		Prior to workshops	Curriculum Director *PCU approves budget*	Budget prepared Submitted to PCU Budget approved
7. Preparation in draft form of detailed syllabus and learning outcomes in core subjects for Grades 1–4 Include objectives, content, methods, resources and evaluation	8 weeks	Began 21 May – complete by end July	CREDU staff assisted by subject matter specialist *Staff available*	Draft syllabus for Grades 1–4 ready for discussion by subject panellists
8. Identification of four schools to participate in		By end of July	Curriculum Director School	Schools for preliminary trial identified

	Activity	Time – venue	Provisional date	Persons involved Critical assumptions	Indicators
	preliminary trialling Contact PEO and school principals School Principals identify 2 teachers to participate from their school			Principals and teachers *Schools and teachers are willing to participate*	Principals and teachers have agreed to participate
9.	Select subject panellists Invite panellists to attend subject panel workshops		By end of July	Curriculum Director, curriculum staff *Panellists willing to attend workshops*	Subject panellists selected
10.	Subject panellists sensitized to new curriculum approach Subject panels discuss draft curriculum format and themes Subject panellists discuss draft syllabus and learning outcomes	2-week workshop (Gambia College)	September	CREDU staff Consultant and subject specialists from USA Subject panellists *Staff, panellists and funding available SMT at DoSE have agreed approach to curriculum*	Subject panellists understand principles of new curriculum Syllabus for core subjects Grades 1–4 agreed
11.	Preparation of sample trial materials for Grade 1	2 weeks (Gambia College)	August	CREDU staff	Sample trial materials for first term of Grade 1 prepared
12.	Grade 1 teachers participating in initial trial to plan	1-week workshop (Gambia College)	October	CREDU staff *Teachers, funding and*	Teachers participating in initial trial able to

	Activity	Time – venue	Provisional date	Persons involved Critical assumptions	Indicators
	implementation of new materials			*staff available; materials returned from printer*	implement trial instructional materials
13.	Initial trial materials for Grade 1 in use in four schools		November	Teachers participating in initial trial *Adequate supply of materials available in school*	Initial trial materials Grade 1 in use in four schools
14.	Complete preparation of trial materials for Grade 1 Begin preparation of Grade 2 material for initial trial		October–December	CREDU staff Team of Lower Basic teachers *Staff available*	Trial materials for Grade 1 completed Preparation of initial trial materials for Grade 2 started
15.	Monitoring of initial trial of Grade 1 materials Develop instruments for monitoring and evaluation of trial testing		November onwards	CREDU staff *Staff and vehicle available*	Regular programme of visits to four schools participating in initial trial established Instruments for monitoring and evaluation of trial testing developed
16.	Revision of trial materials Grade 1 Submit materials for full trial testing to printer	1-week workshop (Gambia College)	January	CREDU staff Subject panellists *Grade 1 trial materials have been*	Trial materials Grade 1 revised and submitted to printer

	Activity	Time – venue	Provisional date	Persons involved Critical assumptions	Indicators
				completed *Staff, panellists* *and funding* *available*	
17.	Train Grade 1 teachers in 15 schools partici-pating in pilot scheme to implement new materials (Total 30 teachers)	1-week workshop (Gambia College)	January 2002	CREDU staff Pilot teachers *Staff and* *teachers* *available* *Materials* *returned from* *printer*	Pilot teachers in 15 schools in Grade 1 able to implement trial materials
18.	Trial materials Grade 1 intro-duced in 15 pilot schools		January 2002	Pilot teachers *Adequate* *supply of* *materials in* *schools*	Full trial testing of Grade 1 and 2 materials begins in 15 pilot schools
19.	Monitoring of trial testing continues		On-going	CREDU staff *Staff and* *vehicle* *available*	Regular monitor-ing of trial testing in 15 pilot schools takes place
20.	Preparation of materials for Grade 2 Submit Grade 2 materials to printer		January–March	CREDU staff Team of Lower Basic teachers *Staff and* *teachers* *available*	Grade 2 materials for trial testing completed and submitted to printer
21.	Review trial testing of Grade 1 materials Revise materials and submit to publisher	1-week workshop + 2 weeks revision	April	CREDU staff Subject panel-lists *Staff, panellists* *and funding* *available*	Grade 1 materials revised and submitted to publisher

	Activity	Time – venue	Provisional date	Persons involved *Critical assumptions*	Indicators
22.	Train Grade 2 teachers partici-pating in trial testing Begin trial testing of Grade 2 materials	1-week workshop	April	CREDU staff Grade 2 teachers	Grade 2 teachers trained to partic-ipate in trial testing Trial testing of Grade 2 materials under way
23.	Begin to prepare trial materials Grades 3 and 4		May–June	CREDU staff Teachers on subject panels *Staff and funding available*	Initial trial materials for Grades 3 and 4 prepared
24.	Training of Grade 1 teachers for full implementa-tion of new materials		Begin July 2002	CREDU staff INSET Regional Training Officers *Staff and funding available*	Lower Basic teachers Grades 1 and 2 able to implement new instructional materials
25.	Review trial testing of Grade 2 materials Revise materials and submit to publisher	1-week workshop + 2 weeks revision	August 2002	CREDU staff Subject panellists *Staff, panellists and funding available*	Grade 2 materials revised and submitted to publisher
26.	New instructional materials intro-duced in Grade 1 throughout country Initial trial testing of Grade 3 and 4 materials in 15 pilot schools		October 2002	CREDU staff Lower Basic teachers Book Production Unit *Adequate supplies of materials printed and dis-tributed to schools*	New instructional materials in Grade 1 in use in all schools Initial trial testing of Grade 3 and 4 materials has begun

THE NEED FOR REFLECTION AND REVIEW

You will by now be very familiar with the idea of experiential learning. If you have been trying out some of the ideas in this book, you will already be gaining some new experiences yourself. In Part I, you were advised to take time for personal reflection as part of your own process of learning and transformation. Just as everyone needs to reflect individually (for example by taking some quiet moments just to think, or even to keep a journal or diary of your own experiences), reflection is also important at an institutional level. This is especially important where innovations or large changes are being introduced.

RECORDING AND SHARING EXPERIENCES

Although reflection and review events are very important, you also need to monitor progress continuously. As we saw earlier, you should take into account the results and outputs of the PCD process, and also the process itself, the context in which it is taking place and of course any impacts which are emerging. You have seen already one example of an action plan which incorporates a monitoring system (page 157).

Another approach is to establish a system of recording experiences which enable you to build up a real picture of what is happening as you go through a period of interventions and change. The information collected through such a system can be used for internal purposes (for a school, for a training institution or for individual teachers and learners) or for external dissemination of what has happened during the PCD cycle. Of course, the use of the information will have to be determined by those people who are closely involved, but it does provide a means of informing relevant stakeholders about what happens, as you may have determined when you made your initial plan for PCD.

An information and experience recording system can comprise three main parts:

1. Table of experience records to be kept
2. Record-keeping action plan: the first table provides the framework for your experience recording, but not how you will do it in practice. So a plan is necessary.
3. Fields for a database: once you collect your information, you need to keep it somewhere, in a filing cabinet, a computer, or somewhere safe. But you will need to put the information into categories (or 'fields'). The types of data you could keep are as follows:

1. Student personal records
   - Name
   - Age
   - Sex
   - Place of origin/home address
   - Key examination marks/grades
   - Details of entrance grades and performance level
   - Comments (issues arising, action taken, result)

2. Teacher personal records
   - Name
   - Age
   - Sex
   - Years of experience
   - Activity with classes

3. Resources used for teaching and learning
   - Facilities used
   - Equipment used
   - Funds used
   - Time used

4. External stakeholders involved in activities related to PCD
   - Name
   - Sex
   - Occupation
   - Place of origin

5. Examination records
   - Examination/tests results
   - Practical skill demonstration results

6. Minutes of meetings and key events relevant to PCD process

As with all the examples in this book, this system is not a blueprint. It is a starting point which you can adapt to suit your own systems, and your own approach to PCD.

A FINAL WORD

This brings us almost to the end of this book on PCD. Hopefully, you will now feel motivated to try some of the ideas and methods you have read about. If you find that you still would like to read more about participatory approaches to education and training, you can find some further references at the end which may be interesting and helpful. Most important, remember that you are as much a learner as the participants in your training courses. If you keep this in mind, you are on the right track to success.

Good luck!

Bibliography

Bao Huy. 'Workshop Results: Review of B.Sc. Forestry Engineer Curriculum Framework at Agricultural and Forestry Faculty'. Tay Nguyen University, 18–19 August, 2000. Buon Me Thuot: Tay Nguyen University, 2000.

Bude, U. *The Process of Curriculum Development. Overcoming 'panic approaches' and ensuring teacher participation.* DSE – Zed Texts. Bonn: DSE, 2000a.

Bude, U. *Curriculum conferences. New directions in curriculum development in Africa.* DSE – Zed Texts. Bonn: DSE, 2000b.

Dang Kim Vui, Dinh Duc Thuan, Hoang Huu Cai and Taylor, P. 'A case study of participatory forestry curriculum development and revision in Vietnam'. In *Forestry Curriculum Development and Revision. Case Studies from Developing Countries.* Rome: FAO, pp. 123–196, 2001.

Dearden, P. 'Participatory Curriculum Development: a Workshop to Update the Forest Guards Course in Nepal'. Rural Development Forestry Network Paper 24d, Winter, 1998.

Freire, P. *The Pedagogy of the Oppressed.* New York: Herder and Herder, 1972.

Helvetas. *Social Forestry Support Programme Project Document.* Hanoi: Swiss Agency for Development and Co-operation and Ministry of Agriculture and Rural Development of the S.R. of Vietnam, September 1997.

Helvetas. '10 key stages towards effective participatory curriculum development – learning from practice and experience in the Social Forestry Support Programme, Vietnam, and other Helvetas-supported projects'. *Experience and Learning in International Cooperation no. 2.* Zurich: Helvetas, 2002.

Hermsen, A. 'Participatory curriculum development in practice. An experience at the Eastern Caribbean Institute for Agriculture and Forestry in Trinidad and Tobago'. In *Sustainable Dimensions*, FAO website. Rome: FAO, 2000.

Kolb, D. *Experiential Learning.* Hemel Hempstead: Prentice-Hall, 1984.

Kroenhart, G. *100 Training Games*. McGraw-Hill, 1997.

Leth, S., Hjortso, N. and Sriskandarajah, N. 'Making the move: a case study in participatory curriculum development in Danish forestry education'. *Journal of Agricultural Education and Extension,* vol. 8, no. 2, 2002.

MARD *Forestry Development Strategy Period 2001–2010*. Hanoi: Government of Vietnam, 2000.

Rogers, A. and Taylor, P. *Participatory Curriculum Development in Agricultural Education. A Training Guide*. Rome: FAO, 1998.

Skilbeck, M. *School Based Curriculum Development*. London: Harper and Row, 1984.

Sotto, E. *When Teaching Becomes Learning. A Theory and Practice of Teaching*. London: Cassell, 1994.

Taylor, P. 'Participatory Curriculum Development – Some Experiences from Vietnam and South Africa', in *Training for Agricultural Development, 1996–98*. Rome: FAO, pp. 4–14, 1998.

Van den Bor, W., Wallace, I., Nagy, G. and Garforth, C. 'Curriculum development in a European context: an account of a collaborative project'. *European Journal of Agricultural Education and Extension,* vol. 2, no. 1, 1995.

Other reading you may find useful

Arnold, R., Burke, B., James, C., Martin, D. and Thomas, B. *Educating for a Change*. Toronto: Between the Lines & Doris Marshall Institute for Education and Action, 1991.

Brookfield, S.D. *Becoming a Critically Reflective Teacher*. San Francisco: Jossey-Bass, 1995.

Chambers, R. *Participatory Workshops*. A sourcebook of 21 sets of ideas and activities. London: Earthscan, 2002.

Harford, N. and Baird, N. *How to Make and Use Visual Aids*. London: VSO/Heinemann, 1997.

Pretty, J., Guijt, I., Thompson, J., and Scoones, I. *Participatory Learning and Action. A Trainer's Guide*. London: IIED, 1995.

Taylor, P. *The Agricultural Science Teachers' Handbook*. London: VSO, 1999.

VSO, IIRR and PEPE. *Creative Training: A User's Guide*. Philippines: VSO Philippines, 1998.

West, E. *201 Icebreakers. Group Mixers, Energizers, and Playful Activities*. New York: McGraw Hill, 1997.

VSO Books

VSO Books publishes practical books and Working Papers in education and development based upon the wide range of professional experience of volunteers and their local partners. Practical Working Papers for teachers and development workers are published on VSO's website for free downloading: www.vso.org.uk

By the same authors:

The English Language Teacher's Handbook, Joanna Baker and Heather Westrup, VSO/Continuum, 174pp, ISBN 0 8264 4787 2.

Books for teachers

The Agricultural Science Teachers' Handbook, Peter Taylor, VSO Books, 148pp, ISBN 0 9509050 7 0

A Handbook for Teaching Sports, National Coaching Foundation, VSO/Heinemann, 160pp, ISBN 0 435 92320 X

How to Make and Use Visual Aids, Nicola Harford, Nicola Baird, VSO/Heinemann, 128pp, ISBN 0 435 92317 X

Introductory Technology – A resource book, Adrian Owens, VSO/ITP, 142pp, ISBN 1 85339 064 X

Life Skills – A training manual for working with street children, Clare Hanbury, VSO/Macmillan, 176pp, ISBN 0 333 95841 1.

The Maths Teachers' Handbook, Jane Portman, Jeremy Richardson, VSO/Heinemann, 108pp, ISBN 0 435 92318 8

The Science Teachers' Handbook, Andy Byers, Ann Childs, Chris Lainé, VSO/Heinemann, 144pp, ISBN 0 435 92302 1

Setting Up and Running a School Library, Nicola Baird, VSO/Heinemann, 144pp, ISBN 0 435 2304 8 4

Books for development workers

Adult Literacy – A handbook for development workers, Paul Fordham, Deryn Holland, Juliet Millican, VSO/Oxfam Publications, 192pp, ISBN 0 85598 315 9

Care and Safe Use of Hospital Equipment, Muriel Skeet and David Fear, VSO Books, 188pp, ISBN 0 9509050 5 4

Diagnosis and Treatment – A training manual for primary health care workers, Dr K Birrell and Dr G Birrell, VSO/Macmillan, 272pp, ISBN 0 333 72211 6.

How to Grow a Balanced Diet, Ann Burgess, Grace Maina, Philip Harris, Stephanie Harris, VSO Books, 244pp, ISBN 0 9509050 6 2

Managing for a Change – How to run community development projects, Anthony Davies, ITP, 160pp, ISBN 1 85339 339 1

Available soon:

Essential Speaking Skills – A handbook for English language teachers, Joanna Baker and Heather Westrup, VSO/Continuum, 2003.

To order and request information about books and discounts, contact:

VSO Books, 317 Putney Bridge Road, London SW15 2PN, UK.
Tel: +44 20 8780 7200 fax: +44 20 8780 7300 e-mail: vsobooks@vso.org.uk

To order online: www.vso.org.uk/vsobooks
VSO promotes volunteering to fight global poverty and disadvantage.
VSO is a registered charity no 313757.

Index